Reader's Digest
Wildlife Watch

Waterside & Coast in Summer

Reader's Digest
Wildlife Watch

Waterside & Coast in Summer

Published by
The Reader's Digest Association Limited
London • New York • Sydney • Montreal

Contents

Wildlife habitats and havens

Animals and plants in focus

Waterside watch

Coast watch

Introduction

There is something mesmerising about water, whether it is the water of a limpid pool, an eddying stream, a cascading torrent, or the relentless, surging sea. In the cold, dark months of winter it can be a forbidding element, inundating the landscape and battering the shore; but in summer, as reflected sunlight flashes from its ripples and waves, it has a magical, calming beauty.

Throughout much of Britain, summer is a season of lush growth. We may curse the clouds that sweep in from the Atlantic, but the rain keeps these islands green. The water that tumbles off the hills flows into streams and rivers, which carry its magic down through farmlands, countryside and cities to the sea.

Looking almost too exotic to be a native British plant, the white water-lily bursts into bloom on ponds, lakes and other quiet freshwaters in July and August.

Summer rainstorms in mid-June often trigger the departure of young frogs from the pools where they developed as tadpoles during the spring.

The delicate little reed warbler has a hard time finding enough food for the giant cuckoo chick that has taken over its nest, killing its rightful occupants.

Enchanted rivers

Streams and rivers are like elongated wildlife reserves, threading through a landscape that has been largely tamed by man. As a result, they are probably the most widely distributed wild habitat in Britain, even though they occupy just one per cent of its area.

Walk down any lowland waterside path in June, and you will see nature in all its exuberant glory. Marginal plants such as common reed, yellow flag iris and reedmace soak up the water and the summer sun, their strong blade-like leaves creating dense stands of vegetation. These shelter nesting birds including the reed bunting and sedge warbler, and conceal other wetland creatures such as the common frog and the elusive water rail. If you are lucky you may even glimpse a water vole nibbling at a reed – a sight that was once common, but is now increasingly rare.

The luxuriance of the water margin extends to the river bank, where the delicate flowers of spring are submerged by a rampant growth of plants that include meadowsweet, willowherb and purple loosestrife. Their flowers attract bees, hoverflies, butterflies and other nectar-feeding insects. Such plants also provide perches for alderflies and mayflies, which have spent most of their lives as aquatic larvae. As adults they survive for only a few days – just long enough to mate and lay their eggs – so they do not need to eat.

By contrast, the damselflies and dragonflies (see pages 73-77) that flutter and dart over the water are dedicated predators. They include powerful aerial hunters such as the emperor dragonfly, fragile creatures such as the azure damselfly, and iridescent dazzlers including the beautiful demoiselle. All these insects glitter like animated jewels as they cling to the vegetation, and if you search around you may find the males and females looped together in their heart-shaped mating embrace, or perhaps flying in tandem as the females lay their eggs.

Wild havens

In some places, such as parts of the Norfolk Broads in East Anglia, networks of rivers and lakes form whole wetland landscapes. Long ago every river had its fringe of marsh and fen; such wetlands are much more

The dazzling monkeyflower, a native of North America, has established itself along many river banks in Britain. Unusually, it flowers in late summer.

The water vole has suffered badly from loss of its streamside habitat, and from predation by introduced American mink that now breed in the wild.

The beautiful painted lady butterfly is a summer visitor from mainland Europe. After flying across the Channel it often settles on coastal flowers to feed.

restricted today, but they still offer a glimpse of a wild waterworld, often dominated by impenetrable vegetation. More importantly, they provide a haven for wetland wildlife that needs more space than can be found in a ribbon of reeds and scrub running alongside a river bank.

On the backwaters of the Broads in summer, you can see rare marshland birds such as the little bearded tit and the magnificent marsh harrier, a bird of prey that patrols low over the reeds in search of voles and frogs. You may also hear the unmistakable song of the cuckoo – an unwelcome sound to many wetland birds such as the reed warbler, which the cuckoo dupes into raising its young. The Broads are the only place in Britain where you can hope to catch sight of the spectacular swallowtail butterfly. Its caterpillars feed on the milk parsley plants that grow in the marshes, and the adults are on the wing in early summer.

Mudflats and salt marsh

Further downstream the river changes its character completely when it comes under the influence of the tidal sea. The intimacy of the river bank is exchanged for the big skies and gleaming mudflats of a broad estuary, and there is a tang of salt in the air. Such places can be bleak indeed in winter, but in summer they are gloriously liberating wildernesses at the fringes of the land.

The rich tidal flats teem with buried molluscs, worms and other marine life, providing plenty of food for birds. By summer the great flocks of overwintering waders and wildfowl have flown north to their summer breeding grounds on the high moorlands and arctic tundra, but at places such as the great estuaries of The Wash in Norfolk and Morecambe Bay in Lancashire there is still plenty to see – especially at high tide, when the rising water pushes the feeding or roosting birds nearer dry land.

Few breeding birds can nest on the tidal flats, but the redshank is an exception. Its chicks are able to float if water floods their nest. The saltmarsh that often develops at the upper spring tide limit is used by breeding oystercatchers, lapwings and shelducks (see pages 60–64), as well as grassland birds such as the skylark and meadow pipit. On Llanrhidian Marsh on the north Gower, south Wales, the birds share the

The colourful striped bill of the puffin is equipped with spines that allow it to carry 20 or more small fish back to the single chick in its clifftop burrow.

Summer-flowering golden samphire is one of the tough, salt-tolerant plants that thrives on the upper levels of salt marshes, shingle banks and rocky cliffs.

Oystercatchers breed on shingle beaches in early summer, relying on the camouflaged shells of their eggs to conceal them among the pebbles.

marsh with half-wild ponies, which still live in herds controlled by stallions that have fought each other for the privilege.

Summer shores

Eventually the river flows out into the sea, and the tidal mudflats of the estuary give way to the sand and shingle beaches of the seashore. In summer these beaches are beautiful places, but they are relatively barren of visible life.

The most interesting areas lie above the high-tide line, where salt-tolerant plants such as sea kale and yellow horned-poppy root among the shingle. The horned-poppy gets its name from the long, horn-like seed capsule that appears after the papery yellow petals have fallen away. The sand dunes that often form behind such beaches are even more intriguing, with distinctive communities of plants and animals that include many rarities (see pages 22–27).

Some of the most rewarding shores for marine life are the rocky coasts of the west and north. The ocean water is clean and full of fish, providing plenty of prey for the vast numbers of sea birds (see pages 28–33) that converge on Britain to breed on the cliffs in early summer. The hard rock at the foot of the cliffs is often eroded into an intricate network of channels and pools, which are colonised by seaweeds and a huge variety of marine animals, including sea anemones, sea snails, barnacles, prawns and crabs. All these animals provide a wealth of food for sea birds.

Rocky shores also sometimes attract mammals such as foxes and stoats, and the more remote coves are used by grey seals. More than 60 per cent of the world's population of grey seals breeds around British coasts, mainly on the rocky shores and islands of the west and north, and they are to be seen on the rocks and in the water throughout the summer. The smaller common or harbour seal favours softer shores, while large numbers breed on the sandy expanses of The Wash in June and July.

Offshore encounters

Continue your journey out to sea – which is highly recommended if you want to see the full splendour of island sea-bird colonies – and you may well have a close encounter with some of the giants of the deep. Each summer huge basking sharks visit the western shores of Britain to graze on the plankton that swarms in the rich coastal waters. You may be lucky enough to fall in with a school of dolphins (see pages 84–88), since they enjoy surfing on the bow waves of boats.

From stream to ocean, the watersides of Britain in summer offer a wonderful wildlife experience that has few equals.

In summer, small octopuses are sometimes trapped in rock pools as the tide goes down. They can change colour to match the rock, so they are hard to see.

The magnificent great green bush cricket needs a mild climate, and it thrives among the scrub on southern sea cliffs where frosts are rare.

The violet-flushed tentacles of the snakelocks anemone are a common sight in rock pools. Unlike many anemones, it cannot retract its tentacles.

Wildlife habitats and havens

- Chalk streams
- In and around the willow tree
- Dunes – life on the shifting sands
- Birdlife on coastal cliffs
- Channel Islands – a cosmopolitan mix

Chalk streams

The tranquil setting of a chalk stream belies the surge in plant and animal life that takes place during the summer, above and below the surface of its sparkling clear water.

A chalk stream starts out as a trickle of clear, cool water bubbling to the surface on a chalky hillside. No matter how far the stream flows, over all sorts of rock, even after widening out into a river, the water always seems to retain its original, sparkling clarity – as long as it is not polluted from an outside source. The chalk rock from which it springs plays an important part in moulding the character of the stream and encouraging the diversity of plants and animals that inhabit it.

Aquifers and springs

Chalk is a sedimentary rock, formed over a hundred million years ago from the shells and skeletons of tiny marine animals. Chalky rocks are found mainly in southern England, where they dominate the landscape as the rolling North and South Downs and Salisbury Plain. The chalk bedrock extends north, through the Chilterns and East Anglia, emerging in the Lincolnshire Wolds and the massive white cliffs at Flamborough Head on the Yorkshire coast.

The chalk rock is porous; rainwater seeps through it and collects in underground cavities known as aquifers. The level of this groundwater forms the local water table. Where the water table rises above the level of any surrounding watertight rocks, the water overflows and gushes out at the surface as a spring. Generally, there are several escape routes for the water along a chalk hillside: each trickle flows gently downhill, joining up to form a network of backwaters and streams that eventually become rivers such as the Avon, the Test, the Wey, the Loddon and the Kennet.

As rainwater percolates through the chalk, any dirt it is carrying is filtered out. After falling through the air and soaking through a layer of

Otters are on the increase but are still a rare sight on the chalk streams of southern England.

LUSH VEGETATION

Plenty of light reaches the stream bed through the clear waters, so water plants thrive wherever there is sand or mud for them to put down roots. water-crowfoot can grow so densely that it has to be cut back to keep the water flowing freely. In a well-managed stream, the rich vegetation provides cover and food for insects, fish and birds, and helps to enrich the oxygen content of the water.

The banks of a chalk stream are packed with plants, too; the leaves of yellow iris, common comfrey and butterbur form dense cover. In summer, domed white flower heads of hemlock and water dropwort and sprays of cream-coloured meadowsweet become perches for damselflies, or demoiselles. Relatives of

the dragonfly, these beautiful and aptly named insects lay their eggs on submerged vegetation. Banded demoiselles flutter among the bankside plants; the almost circular deep blue patch on each wing of the male gives him a butterfly-like appearance in flight.

The bright pink flowers of great willowherb add to the dazzling array of colours stippling the margins of the stream throughout the summer.

▲Yellow irises grow at the edge of streams. This particular species can also thrive in the water where it flows slowly.

◄Banded damselflies are widespread, but localised, in the south. You see them basking on leaves hanging over the water.

◄Water-crowfoot is mostly submerged in water – only its flowers break the surface.

The chalk-stream landscape looks blissfully tranquil; the bright, shallow water flows gently over submerged plants and between overgrown banks. Together the clear water and profusion of plants create a healthy and nourishing environment for many birds, fish and invertebrates.

► Chalk streams contain plenty of dissolved minerals, including calcium, which molluscs such as this water snail need to build strong shells.

◄ Crustaceans, such as these freshwater shrimps, moult regularly and use the calcium dissolved in the stream's water to replace their shells.

topsoil, rainwater is also slightly acid. As a result, it dissolves some of the the chalk, and the calcium-rich water is stored in the aquifer until it gurgles to the surface as a clean, cool spring.

Vulnerable habitat

As the young, fast-flowing chalk stream tumbles along, it throws water up into the air where it absorbs oxygen. The turbulence also increases the evaporation rate that helps to keep the water cool. Cold water carries more dissolved oxygen than warm water and the combined effect of splashing and cooling means that chalk streams usually have a high oxygen content. This supports a wide range of aquatic molluscs, insect larvae and fish that would struggle to survive elsewhere. However, it also means that pollution or warming of the water will have a serious effect on the sensitive creatures that live in the stream.

Certain chalk streams have always had a tendency to disappear in dry summers when the water table drops and the springs stop running. This problem has been exacerbated by the extraction

▲ Brown trout thrive in chalk streams, on a diet of adult and larval mayflies.

◀ Even on a leaf beside the stream, a mayfly may not be out of the reach of a leaping brown trout. Mayflies proliferate in chalk streams because their aquatic larvae (nymphs) need the oxygen-rich waters to survive.

of water from underground aquifers for human consumption, to irrigate crops or to water livestock. Many chalk streams that formerly kept flowing now regularly dwindle to a trickle in summer or break up into shallow, stagnant pools, which warm up easily and are low in oxygen. Such loss of habitat and oxygen starvation kills

▲ Minnows are found in clean, cool shallows with stony bottoms, where shoals of them feed many fish and birds.

◄ Grey herons seek out slower-moving stretches of water, and often stand motionless, poised to strike at passing fish.

forming a powerful seal that anchors it firmly to its base so it cannot move far. The little mollusc feeds by filtering tiny food particles out of the water; its delicate feeding apparatus would soon become clogged with sediment in a muddy river, but in the clear waters of a chalk stream it flourishes.

Small fish and insects attract birds to the stream. Little grebes nest in the dense cover of reeds and sedges along the river banks and feed on small fish, such as minnows and nine-spined sticklebacks, that hug the shallows. Grey herons stalk these shallow waters, striking at any unsuspecting fish that swim within range. Large rocks in the middle of the stream provide convenient perches from which grey wagtails can snatch at the insects flying above the water.

Most fish hunt insects, too. The mottled-brown bullhead is well camouflaged as it lies among the gravel on the

many tiny inhabitants of the stream and has a knock-on effect throughout the whole community. This is one of the most critical and urgent problems that needs to be addressed in the management of Britain's water resources.

Clear signs

The tiny river limpet is a good indicator of how clean the stream water really is. The soft edge of its shell clings to the surface of a rock or leaf,

---

The most picturesque chalk streams have an abundance of reeds, sedges and irises lining their banks. These plants support innumerable insects, some of which fall off into the water, where fish quickly gulp them down.

WATERFRONT RESIDENTS

Low, overhanging branches cast dappled shade and also provide convenient perches from which kingfishers can watch for fish in the clear water below. For all its brightness, the kingfisher is hard to see as it flashes up and down the stream or darts in and out of trees on the bank: its vibrant, iridescent colouring is good camouflage against the shimmering water. Listen out for a quiet splash and you may see a kingfisher coming out of the water with

a small fish in its beak. Or you may catch a glimpse of one preening itself on a twig.

Look out for holes in the high sand banks beside the stream. A pair of kingfishers usually raise their young in a tunnel, which they excavate with their feet and beaks, well above the swirling water to avoid flooding.

Water voles are shy and scarce, so all you may see or hear of them is a faint ripple and quiet splash as they slip

◄ Kingfishers favour chalk streams because the small fish they feed upon are abundant in the shallows and easy to see in the clear water.

▲ A water vole feeds mostly on plants at the water's edge, where it is in constant danger of being taken by predatory mink and grey herons.

in and out of the water. They burrow among the roots of willows and alders in the soft banks of the stream to create a maze of tunnels. There is usually at least one underwater entrance, so the water voles can come and go unseen.

Many voles fall prey to the voracious mink, a newcomer to the environment. You are more likely to see a mink beside most streams than you are the rare and elusive otter.

stream bed, waiting for aquatic insect larvae to come past. The caddis-fly larva conceals itself from hungry predators by building a case of gravel chippings around its body so that it merges into the background.

An occasional splash in the water could be a brown trout snatching insects from the surface. Native brown trout are very elusive, even though the large purple spots on their flanks make them easy to identify. It is probably best to look for them when they congregate to spawn in the gravelly shallows in autumn. The spawning trout are often joined by hungry grayling, which feed greedily on any eggs that drift into open water.

Brown trout find mayflies irresistible and eat as many as they can catch. There are about 50 different species of mayfly in Britain, although all look similar and share a similar life cycle. The larval stage of the mayfly is a three-tailed nymph, which is totally aquatic. It may live and feed among the plants and gravel of a chalk stream for as long as three years. Mayfly nymphs are sensitive to pollution, so their presence in a stream is another sign that the waterway is in good health.

SECRETS OF THE WATERCRESS BED

Watercress is a plant that likes to grow in or beside shallow, running water. It has been harvested from the ditches and chalk streams of lowland Britain for centuries. Up until now, careful management of the watercress beds has kept the chalk streams flowing all year round, relatively unaffected by low rainfall, except in a serious drought. The temperature of the water remains more or less constant, so the beds rarely freeze. In the most extreme winters, the spring water may be several degrees warmer than the surrounding air temperature, providing a stable habitat, perfect for a variety of invertebrates, birds and one small mammal, the water shrew.

Beneath the surface, freshwater shrimps teem in their thousands. These little crustaceans feed on the remains of dead animals and rotting vegetation that accumulate in the slower flowing parts of the stream. Other crustaceans called water lice, or slaters, and bloodworms are also abundant.

Moorhens swim up and down the shallow streams, flicking their white tails and snatching at these small invertebrates, which live among the lush foliage. In winter, when many of the surrounding waterways start to freeze, the watercress bed provides a refuge for a shy bird called the water rail. The bird is rarely seen, but often heard: its cry is a pig-like squeal. Occasionally, the rail emerges from the dense vegetation to feed on the insects and snails among the watercress.

Another bird, the snipe, is a wader that is difficult to see as it stands among tall vegetation, although its plump, brown body stands out against the bright green watercress. It probes the mud under the watercress with its extremely long, thin bill, looking for worms.

In spring and autumn, the watercress bed provides migrating birds, such as green sandpipers, with invaluable service stations. Here they can refuel before flying on to their breeding grounds in northern Europe or their wintering sites in the Mediterranean and Africa.

The water shrew is in its element in the watercress beds. It swims through the water and scurries busily through the lush vegetation, finding a plentiful supply of freshwater shrimps, aquatic insect larvae, small snails, worms, young frogs and little fish to eat.

◀ **Water rails are widespread and relatively common, yet rarely seen because of their secretive habits. The rich pickings in watercress beds may tempt one out into the open.**

▼ **Deeper chalk streams support mute swans, attracted by the abundant aquatic vegetation on which they feed.**

Watercress grows in clear, shallow, unpolluted streams. It flowers from early summer into autumn.

The mass emergence of adult mayflies on warm, muggy evenings from May to August is a spectacular sight. It begins with the nymphs hauling themselves clear of the water, then moulting – sometimes twice – to emerge as winged adults. As soon as their wings are fully inflated with blood, they take to the air in vast mating swarms, dancing above the stream. The flight period of a mayfly generally lasts just a few hours, during which time many are caught by predators. In any case, the males die shortly after mating, and the females after laying their eggs in the water.

In recent years, there have been massive declines in the number of mayflies emerging each year on the main fishing rivers, such as the River Test in Hampshire. The reasons for this are not clear – pollution is just one possible cause.

Lurking in the shadows

Bigger predatory fish hang around in the deep pools carved out by the eddying waters on meandering stretches of the stream. There they wait among the tangled roots of alder and willows. Large trout and chub that are too big to cruise the shallows loiter behind tree roots and rocks in more turbulent waters. Chub take any morsel that passes within reach, from a plump caterpillar blown off an overhanging branch to an unwitting minnow or a young trout separated from its shoal.

Large perch also patrol the overgrown margins of the stream looking for smaller fish, worms and crustaceans. Their greenish scales and dark vertical bands provide the perfect camouflage for a fish that relies on ambushing its prey from dense cover. In the deepest pools lurks the pike, the top predator of the chalk stream. With its long, muscular body and powerful jaws, a large pike can prey on other fish, including roach, dace and trout, on frogs, ducklings, moorhen chicks and even water voles.

One of the strangest residents of the chalk stream is the brook lamprey, a primitive, jawless fish-like creature that spends most of its life as a juvenile, buried in the mud on the stream bed, filtering food particles from the water. After five or six years, it emerges as an adult. Its eel-like body is about 15cm (6in) long and about as thick as a pencil with a row of gill openings but no fins or scales. An adult brook lamprey never feeds; instead of a mouth it has a sucker for anchoring itself to rocks.

From mid-April to late June, adult lampreys migrate upstream to spawn in the clean gravel beds. On hatching, the young are swept downstream again where they burrow into the mud.

The shy green sandpiper flies south for winter, but breaks its journey to spend July to September in England, feeding mainly on the shrimps in chalk streams. A few stop off again in spring on their way back north.

▲ Pike rely on sight to spot their prey, so the clear waters of a chalk stream are a perfect hunting ground. The abundance of marginal plants also offers plenty of cover.

▶ An adult brook lamprey uses its large sucker to move stones on the bed of a chalk stream to form a chamber in which to lay its eggs.

WILDLIFE WATCH

Where can I explore chalk streams?

● The best chalk streams are found in the south and south-east of England. However, there is one small snag: many are among the most prized fishing streams in Britain, and trespassers are not welcome. Always seek permission before entering private land, or stick to public areas and official footpaths.

● The rivers and streams around Hungerford in Berkshire are prime examples of the chalk-stream habitat.

● The Rivers Test and Itchen in Hampshire are two of the finest chalk rivers. The Test is best seen near Romsey. The Hampshire Avon close to Fordingbridge is also good.

● In Dorset, the River Frome, between Dorchester and Wareham, is excellent chalk-stream territory and even has salmon living in it.

● There are short stretches on the River Darent in Kent and along the upper reaches of the River Wey in Surrey where you can find typical chalk-stream plants and animals. These sites are liable to dry up in summer when water is being drawn off upstream to irrigate crops and refresh livestock.

In and around the willow tree

Famous as the source of wood for making cricket bats, the living willow is an intrinsic part of the waterside scenery where it provides a home for a multitude of insects and animals, and even other plants that take root on its rugged bark.

Graceful willows are a familiar sight along the banks of many rivers and streams. On hot summer days, their spreading branches and soft green leaves provide welcome shade for fishermen, as well as for cattle grazing in riverside fields.

Generally, willows are inhabitants of wet soils. As well as growing along watercourses, they are found on the shores of lakes and ponds, in fens and marshes and in the waterlogged soils of heaths, moorlands and mountains.

There are many different species of willow. These vary in size from the diminutive dwarf willow, which grows on mountains and is only a few centimetres in height, to the majestic crack and white willows, which can soar to a height of around 25m (80ft). The picture is complicated by numerous natural hybrids and specially reared cultivars. It is often difficult to find a pure-bred willow in areas where two freely interbreeding species coexist. The cricket-bat willow is the most famous hybrid: a cross between white willow and crack willow, its wood is tough but light and elastic.

Waterside giants

On the whole, the larger willows support the greatest abundance of wildlife. Some crack and white willows are left to grow naturally to their full height, but it is far more common for these large willows to be pollarded. This involves cutting their main branches back to the trunk, to encourage rapidly growing new shoots to sprout around the top.

The common long-eared bat feeds by hovering among the branches of willow trees, gleaning insects from the leaves. It roosts in tree holes during the summer.

Pollarding willows creates wounds that are open to fungal infection. As a result, willow trees are often riddled with rot holes and their trunks may even be hollow. Such cavities are important habitats for wildlife. Bats roost in the hollow trunks; owls and jackdaws may nest there. Shelducks and wood ducks build their nests on the platform at the top of a

As willows like to have their roots in water, they are frequently found growing beside rivers and streams. In fact, they are often planted there deliberately, since their roots help to stabilise vulnerable banks.

CRACK WILLOW FACT FILE

The crack willow is one of the largest and most widely distributed species of willow in the country. It grows beside rivers and streams in lowland valleys; north of Perth in Scotland it is more likely to have been planted than it is to be growing naturally. The crack willow may have been introduced to Ireland, too, since its distribution there is patchy.

● NAMES
Common name: crack willow
Scientific name: *Salix fragilis*

● HEIGHT
Grows to a maximum of about 25m (80ft)

● LIFE SPAN
Tens of years rather than hundreds due to a weakness in trunk, which often cracks open and rots

● TRUNK AND BRANCHES
Mature trees have short, thick trunks and long main branches rising from trunk no more than 3m (10ft) above ground; often pollarded, so natural shape is lost; fully mature specimens are rare, since trunks tend to rot from centre, especially after pollarding; despite such damage, trees can survive for decades

● BARK
Smooth and green on young twigs, deeply furrowed and dark grey on old trees

● LEAVES
Glossy green and pointed; up to 15cm (6in) long and 5–9 times longer than they are broad; turn yellow then brown in autumn

● BUDS
Brown, flattened oval with single outer bud scale

● FLOWERS
Catkins, 6–7cm (2½–2¾in) long, appear at same time as leaves; male catkins (yellow) and smaller female catkins (green) on separate trees; each catkin bears many individual flowers, which produce nectar to attract insect pollinators; also uses wind pollination

● FRUITS
After pollination, fertilised female flowers mature into white, woolly fruit – fluffy-haired seeds are blown along by wind

● USES
Traditionally trimmed (pollarded) regularly to produce young, pliant branches for fencing and hurdles, basketmaking and weaving lobster pots; bark was used in tanning of hides to make leather

Willow leaves are generally oval in outline, those of crack willow being particularly narrow and elongated.

A mature and healthy crack willow has a broadly domed outline, with the main branches originating from fairly low down on the trunk.

The twigs of crack willow snap easily and readily root in the ground.

Grey willow grows as large shrubs in damp habitats, including fens and boggy woodland. A mass of catkins is produced in the spring, at about the same time as the leaves begin to appear. The catkins are pollinated by swarms of insects, particularly bumblebees. The leaves are the foodplant for the caterpillars of numerous moths.

WILLOW OR SALLOW?

In old books about trees, the name sallow was often used instead of willow for some species. Sallow was just a country name for willow, derived from the scientific name *Salix*, but it is no longer an official botanical name. It was most frequently applied to *Salix caprea*, which, at one time or another, has been called great sallow, goat willow and pussy willow – goat willow is now its accepted name. The most common willow, now known as the grey willow, used to be called the common sallow or fen sallow.

Goat willow is common and widespread. Its egg-shaped leaves are eaten by many kinds of insects, most notably the caterpillars of the purple emperor butterfly.

◄ **A gaping hole in a rotten willow trunk makes an ideal nesting site for the little owl. When a little owl chick is nearly ready to fly, it climbs up and spends the day sitting outside the hole.**

◄**Wood ducks and shelducks nest on top of a willow's trunk, so their ducklings must start life by leaping to the ground shortly after hatching. The wood duckling here has spread its tiny wings and webbed feet for a parachute effect to soften the landing.**

pollarded trunk; another duck, the mallard, nests inside the trunk as long as there is a suitable access hole at the base of the tree. Great tits and blue tits use the smaller holes for their nests, and the treecreeper often nests under loose bark on the trunk.

Close neighbours
A number of small plants actually grow on willow trees. There may be a green shadow of moss on the thicker branches, while some ferns and flowering plants sprout from the humus in the deep furrows of the bark. Dead leaves that collect in the deeper cracks, and especially

in the tops of pollarded willows, rot down to form the humus. In some areas, particularly in the Severn Vale, the parasitic mistletoe is found clinging to willow trees.

A few wildflowers share the willow's liking for damp roots. Brooklime, with its small, bright blue flowers, common comfrey, a great favourite with bumblebees, and purple loosestrife thrive in the moist earth around the base of a willow tree.

Under attack
In the summer, most willow trees, especially the pollarded ones, are assaulted by a horde of voracious insects, looking for food and somewhere to lay their eggs. It is amazing that some willows have any whole or unblemished leaves left by the end of the summer, given the legions of insects that feast

on them. Many kinds of moth caterpillars nibble on willow leaves, unperturbed by their bitterness, including the spectacular puss moth caterpillar with its strange, intimidating 'facial' markings and whip-like lashing 'tails'. The names of other moths, such as the sallow kitten and sallow clearwing, reflect their food preferences in the old name for willow.

The leaves of willows may be festooned with little groups of willow sawfly larvae, neatly spaced around the leaf edges. When disturbed, they simultaneously cock their tails in the air, which makes them easy to see.

The red-tipped clearwing moth's caterpillar feeds on willows, too, although it lives out of sight inside the stems. It prefers regularly pollarded willow trees, where the regrowing branches are approximately 2–3cm (¾–1¼in) in diameter and still tender and juicy. Several clearwing caterpillars are often found feeding close together inside the same stem.

◄ **Common comfrey, which flowers during May and June, is traditionally highly valued by herbalists.**

▼ **Brooklime, a kind of speedwell frequently found clustered around the base of willows, is in flower from May to September.**

▼ **Pollarded specimens of white willow grow so rapidly and vigorously that their crowns are thick and bushy, with branches more than 2m (6ft 6in) long, just a few months after being cut back.**

DID YOU KNOW?
The willow has long been known to have healing properties. When malaria still existed in Britain, willow branches used to be taken into the patient's room to help treat the disease.

Traditionally, country people drank infusions of the leaves to treat aches and pains and fevers, and perhaps surprisingly this is not too far from what we do today. Willow leaves contain a substance called salicin, which gives them their bitter taste. From this, chemists developed salicylic acid, the main ingredient of aspirin, which is still one of the most widely used analgesics for alleviating aches and fevers.

FUNGI ON WILLOWS

Many large willows are host to the blushing bracket fungus. The tough, fleshy brackets are 3–8cm (1¼–3¼in) wide and several often sprout, one above the other, from dying

◀ Blushing bracket fungus is commonly found on willow trees. Here, it is growing out in tiers from the rotting trunk of a silver birch tree.

branches. The upper surface is zoned in bands of brown and pale pink at first but, as its name suggests, these often turn a deeper red with age and when bruised.

The willow pluteus, *Pluteus salicinus*, is common on willow trees, stumps and logs. Its dark grey cap has a greenish tinge and is carried on a slender pale greenish stem. It is sometimes closely associated with clusters of the attractive *Pholiota alniola*, which is rarely found far from damp alder or willow woodlands. The golden brown caps are rather sticky and become wavy round the edges as they get older.

The most abundant fungus on willow logs and stumps is the crumble-cap, *Coprinus*

disseminatus. Hundreds of these small greyish fungi are often found crammed cap-to-cap on a suitable stump. The cap is just 1–2cm (½–¾in) in diameter, deeply grooved and very fragile, crumbling when touched. The gills of the crumble-cap get slightly darker as the cap matures but, unlike many ink-cap fungi, seldom spontaneously disintegrate into an inky, slimy goo.

The scarlet elf cup likes rich damp soils with moss and rotting wood. This is one of the few fungi to be found in midwinter and very early spring and is particularly striking when nestling in a bed of green moss. Only the inside of the cup is smooth and scarlet, the outside is brownish white and softly downy.

Beetles and bugs

It can get quite crowded inside young willow stems during the summer. The larvae of the willow weevil are also occupants of the stems, eating their way up the underside of the bark and producing telltale brown, ulcerated spots. The grey and white adult weevil is a humpbacked, wrinkled creature that looks like a natural swelling low down on the bark of the slender young stems. The spotted willow aphid likes sucking the plant's sap through the thin, soft bark of the new shoots.

The larvae of the musk beetle, a large longhorn beetle, munch on decaying timber. The adult is a bright metallic green, sometimes tinged with a coppery or blue sheen. In July and August, it is found on willow leaves and other riverside plants. It is especially fond of hogweed, angelica and meadowsweet flowers, where it sits for hours, sipping nectar.

Bumps and blisters

By high summer it can be hard to find a willow leaf that is not covered with numerous small swellings called galls. These growths are the willow tree's way of isolating the parasitic larvae of various mites and insects living inside them to minimise the damage they can do. The most common, the bean gall, is caused by a sawfly. Crack willow is its favourite host; a single long leaf can have ten or more wrinkled red blisters bulging above and below its surface, each with a single larva feeding inside. A gnat larva irritates the tree into forming a cluster of leaves at the tip of

▲ Decaying stumps of various willow species frequently support densely stacked colonies of the delicate, pleated crumble-cap toadstool, or fairies' bonnets as they are quaintly called.

▶ In late autumn and early winter, a search among the moss growing under willow trees may reveal clusters of scarlet elf cups, which look like tiny curled up pieces of orange peel.

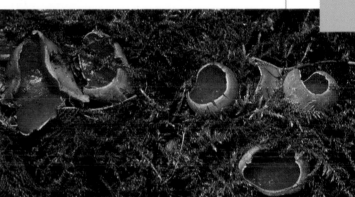

the stem in which it is hiding. The mass of leaflets looks like the petals of a flower, so it is called the camellia or rosette gall. One large brown froghopper uses willow. Its larva is a type of 'cuckoo-spit' insect – it feeds on sap under a froth of foam, which bubbles out from its rear end.

▲ Puss moth caterpillars chew their way through the leaves of willows. Although more than 2.5cm (1in) long, they are hard to see among the greenery.

◀ Musk beetles are associated with ancient willows, since their larvae feed on decaying timber.

WILDLIFE WATCH

Where can I find willow trees?

● Goat willow, *Salix caprea*, is the well-known pussy willow with its furry male catkins and oval leaves. It is widespread and less dependent on wet soil than other willows.

● Creeping willow, *Salix repens*, rarely exceeds 30cm (12in) in height although it may trail along the ground for a metre or more. It grows on wet heaths and in bogs, fens and damp dune hollows.

● Bay-leaved willow, *Salix pentandra*, is found north of a line from north Wales to York. It grows 18m (60ft) high and has glossy deep green leaves that are oval in shape.

Dunes – life on the shifting sands

From a distance, dunes may look like desolate heaps of sand but closer investigation reveals a wealth of life that is perfectly adapted to this exposed and unstable habitat.

The tiny pale flowers of the rue-leaved saxifrage, a self-pollinated annual, brighten the dunes from April to June.

On the front line between land and sea, sand dunes are among the most inhospitable places to live anywhere in Britain. Baked by the summer sun, the sand can be as hot and dry as a desert; in a storm, the dunes are sprayed with salty sea water and lashed by strong winds. Yet this unpromising environment is remarkably rich in wildlife.

The kind of plants and animals that colonise dunes depends on the local sand. For instance, in areas where the sand is composed primarily of the crushed shells of long-dead molluscs, conditions are very alkaline and the flora is dominated by a specialised group of lime-loving plants.

Drifting sands

The biggest and best dunes in Britain are those down the west coast, where the prevailing wind blows onshore, so the sand piles up faster than it is washed or blown away again.

To understand how a dune system forms and evolves into a switchback of sandy hummocks and hollows, take a walk straight inland from the open beach, crossing over the dunes, until there is no more sand under your feet.

Just behind the beach, you will see the dunes start to blister the landscape. At first there are just a few little piles of wind-blown sand trapped in spiky tufts of marram grass. These are embryo dunes.

NATIONAL RARITIES

Sand dunes are good places to go looking for two reptiles: the common lizard and the sand lizard. The common lizard is found on most dunes, but only a few on the south Lancashire coast have sand lizards living on them as well.

The sand lizard is common across Europe, but it has reached the northern limit of its range in Britain. Here its distribution is restricted to heaths in Dorset and Surrey, and to sand dunes on Merseyside.

The sand lizard basks on warm patches of sand, never far from shelter. At the first hint of danger it scuttles off to hide among the nearest plants. These lizards feed on the insects attracted by the dry warmth of the sand. The female digs holes in the loose sand in which to lay her eggs. Adult sand lizards sometimes prey on young of their own species as well as those of the common lizard.

Another rarity found on dunes is the natterjack toad. As an amphibian, the natterjack seeks out the moist, shady dips between the dunes where it can avoid being dried out by the winds or baked by the scorching sun and sand.

The green tinge on the flanks of a male sand lizard spreads and becomes brighter in the breeding season.

The rare natterjack toad finds the damp, sheltered hollows among the dunes to its liking, even though the water is slightly salty. There are plenty of insects on the dunes for the natterjack to eat.

Marram grass binds the dunes together with its extensive network of roots. Repeatedly engulfed by moving sands, its tough leaves keep pushing their way back through.

A creeping perennial frequently found on sand dunes, sea bindweed also grows on sandy shores and in fine shingle. In flower from June to August, it is often pollinated by bumblebees.

A few other plants join the battle to subdue the wanderings of these fore-dunes. Broad mats of sea sandwort, with its fleshy yellow-green leaves, hold on tight alongside sea and Portland spurges, which have pale green shiny leaves. Apart from these hardy colonisers, however, the fore-dunes are too unstable to harbour much in the way of wildlife.

Grass roots

Just a little farther inland are the grey dunes, where the sand becomes carpeted with lichens and mosses – their colour gives these dunes their name. Conditions here become unsuitable for the marram grass, which is gradually replaced by a different selection of plants, adapted to more stable soils.

The two plants that play the main roles in changing a shifting yellow dune to a fixed grey one are red fescue grass and sand sedge. Their rhizomes interweave to form an intricate network that finally puts a stop to the sand's drifting habits. This is where you find the prickly leaved grey-green sea holly with its pompoms of tiny blue flowers. Sea bindweed is another true dune plant. Its pink trumpet flowers and fleshy leaves are borne on creeping stems that grow from a mesh of sand-stabilising rhizomes.

The fixed dunes are where the majority of plants and

They move with the wind and re-form after being washed away by the highest tides.

Beyond the embryo dunes are the fore-dunes. These are much higher and are known as yellow dunes. Here, the sand is still loose and liable to be lifted up by the wind and blown inland over the crest of the dune.

Sand traps

The key to the whole formation of dunes is the marram grass, which breaks the force of the wind so that the sand grains settle among its stalks. It has an extensive root system and a network of buried rhizomes (creeping stems) that effectively bind the restless sand grains together. Lyme grass and sea couch grass assist, but they cannot keep on doggedly pushing their way through repeated smotherings of sand like the stalwart marram grass does.

▶ Sea holly grows just above the high watermark of spring tides. A perennial, it flowers from June to September.

◀ The wild pansy grows freely on sand and shingle beaches. It flowers from spring to autumn and is pollinated by bees.

animals are found. Some of the commonest flowers, such as ragwort and hound's tongue, have long tap-roots. These anchor the plants in the sand and seek out well-buried water to sustain them through the warm, dry summer months.

Flower shows

The dainty red-leaved fingered saxifrage avoids dying from thirst by flowering early. Its tiny white flowers blossom on cool April days. It has fruited and died by the end of May, leaving its hardy seeds to withstand the heat and drought of summer. The white-flowered mouse-ear chickweeds, whitlow grass and early forget-me-not, with its tiny sky-blue flowers, have similar flowering strategies. The delicate yellow flowers of the seaside pansy also shun the summer heat and add welcome colour to the dunescape in April and May.

The domed, lace-like white flower heads of the sea carrot are scattered almost everywhere from June onwards. They are a great favourite of the sulphur dune beetle, which occurs in its thousands on some dunes. In early summer, extravagant displays of kidney vetch bloom

◄ Sandhill snails are often found clustered together, waiting out the hot, dry days of summer with their shells sealed by a layer of mucus.

on some dunes; the flowers can be pink, red or white instead of the usual yellow. Its leaves are eaten by caterpillars of the common blue butterfly and the five and six-spot burnet moths. The gaudy black and red adult moths adorn yellow ragwort in July.

▶ Poplar leaf beetles look like ladybirds without their spots.

Insect life

Butterflies and moths are scarce on most dunes. The dark green fritillary may drop in for a quick sip from a hawkbit flower head. Grass eggar moth caterpillars toil across the sands in search of somewhere to pupate.

The dune snail beetle eats snails alive inside their shells. This shiny black beetle usually seeks out sandhill snails, which encrust the stems and leaves of plants such as sea carrot. Stems may bend under the sheer weight of the snails.

Robber flies love hot, dry places, so dunes suit them well. They often stop to bask on the paths, flying up when disturbed and landing a short distance away. They prey on a variety of insects, including each other, and often attack therevid flies, truly coastal insects, the males of which have a splendid dense pelt of silver hair.

Moist hollows

The damp troughs in between the dunes are called slacks and are often where the most interesting plants grow, as they are more sheltered and stable than the shifting dune-tops. Moisture and nutrients

▲ Robber flies are large and strongly built, with powerful legs. They have a horny proboscis; with this long, tubular mouthpiece they pierce their insect prey and suck out the juices.

◄ This early marsh-orchid grows in the wet hollows among the sand known as dune slacks. In some localities it grows by the thousand. It flowers during May and June.

trickling down through the sand collects there, creating fertile oases between the heaps of desert-like sand.

Creeping willow thrives in the slacks of some of Britain's larger west coast dune systems. It is often heavily attacked by the shiny black and red poplar leaf beetle. Bog pimpernel also carpets the slacks. Its myriad dainty pink bell-shaped flowers arise from slender trailing stems hidden among the wet grass and moss.

The dune slacks are home to a specialised wetland flora that includes numerous orchids. The rare fen orchid crops up on some western dunes, while in some areas there may be hundreds of thousands of marsh helleborine. The tall purple spires of the southern marsh-

PROTECTED!

Many of Britain's sand dunes are considered internationally important habitats. They are consequently afforded various degrees of statutory protection.

◄ The sandy, well-drained soils on the oldest dunes are good places for rabbits to dig their burrows. By nibbling the grassy swards, the rabbits produce close-cropped turf, which they litter with droppings.

◄ Burnet moths are widespread and conspicuous in summer. They live in colonies, and their bright colours warn birds that they are all poisonous.

▲ There are two species of spurge bug in Britain. This one is commonly found on southern and western coasts.

that they often become covered in dense thickets of privet, ivy and other woody plants that squeeze out everything else.

Haven for wildlife

As soon as there is more permanent cover, rabbits start colonising the dunes. They emerge from their warrens to nibble the tender herbs and grasses. Some dunes are so well grazed by rabbits that the only plants that manage to flower are the less palatable ones, such as viper's bugloss.

An undisturbed dune system is teeming with wildlife. A common lizard may scramble across the path in front of you, its feet sinking ankle-deep into the soft sand. The trilling of a meadow pipit may ring out across the dunes; its nest is probably tucked away at the base of a marram tuft somewhere nearby. The rapturous song of a soaring skylark may cause you to look up momentarily to try to find the source of the breathless melody. Jackdaws commute from their nests on any nearby crags to probe in the sand for insects.

Some dune systems, mainly on the east coast, are home to noisy nesting colonies of terns for half the year, from

April to October. They are most likely to be common terns, which breed in a variety of coastal habitats, but little terns can also be seen, for example in north Norfolk. You may also have to watch your step to avoid treading on the beautifully camouflaged eggs of the oystercatcher, partly concealed in a shallow scrape in the sand.

Northern dune systems may play host to the

orchid tower over the squat, thick-stemmed early marsh-orchid, which is a striking brick-red colour on sand dunes. Dune slacks are not the only place to find orchids on the dunes. Pyramidal and bee orchids and the white-flowered autumn-lady's-tresses are often found in the drier spots.

At their farthest point inland, the dunes are so stable

The elegant common tern nests in dense colonies on the coast, often among vegetation on the dunes, but also on the open sand. Terns are most vocal while breeding in mid-May.

DUNE BEES AND WASPS

Dunes are a favourite haunt for a number of bees and hunting wasps. The little silvery-grey females of the silver leaf-cutter bee fly in carrying their neatly carved sections of leaf. They drop down and scurry into their burrows, which are often closely packed on flat or gently sloping areas of stable dune. The seaside leaf-cutter is a much larger reddish brown bee that also nests in the sand, as do many other solitary bees and wasps.

Insect nest building starts early. In April on some of the western dunes, huge numbers of the creeping willow bee are swinging into action. Time is of the essence, because the only plant that the female bees visit to collect nectar and pollen is the creeping willow, which has quite a brief and early flowering period.

▲ The silver leaf-cutter bee feeds on the nectar and pollen of plants, such as restharrow, and cuts neat semicircles out of leaves to build the walls of her nest.

▼ The leaden spider wasp has very long legs so it can straddle the body of a spider and drag it across the sand.

The little dune snail bee builds her nest-cells in the dry and spacious vault of an empty snail shell. She provisions each chamber with nectar and pollen on which she lays her eggs. Then she seals up the shell by chewing leaves into a sort of sticky putty that she spreads over the opening. Next time you are wandering across dunes, try not to tread on snail shells as they could be sheltering bee nurseries.

The sand wolf spider divides its time between its burrow and the open sands, where its colouring is good camouflage until it moves. Then it may meet a nasty end if a hunting wasp that specialises in tracking down these spiders happens to be passing. The leaden spider wasp is often seen dragging a

paralysed spider across the dune. The wasp then digs a burrow in the sand, deep enough to take the spider and the egg that it will lay on the spider's helpless, limp body. As the spider is there to provide food for the wasp larva, it is only immobilised, not killed, so that it will stay fresh until the larva has eaten it alive. A long, slender sand digger wasp may be seen trundling over the sand with a huge caterpillar, bigger than itself, slung beneath its body. This heavy burden receives the same treatment as the spider, and for the same purpose. Many sand dunes are a paradise for various species of hunting wasp, each one homing in on its own particular kind of victim.

▼ Following in the tradition of the hermit crab, which moves into a discarded whelk shell to protect its naked body, the dune snail bee uses an empty snail shell as a crèche for her larvae.

► Common and well camouflaged in the sand, wolf spiders prey on the many insects living on the dunes.

Dunes are often located behind popular and accessible beaches. This offers ample opportunity for exploration, but make sure you stick to the paths and do not damage this fragile habitat by trampling it underfoot.

The mottled brown eider duck sits patiently on her nest, incubating four to six greenish grey eggs in a bed of eiderdown plucked from her own breast.

eider duck. The female relies on her camouflage to protect her while she is incubating her eggs. She sits very closely and is almost trodden on before deserting her post. Usually, several eider ducks nest side by side; in the colony there are often a few non-breeding aunty ducks who help to look after the ducklings once they have hatched.

When covered in gorse and heather, the tops of the oldest dunes are often very heath-like in appearance, and the wildlife on dunes and sandy heaths has much in common. For any animal or plant living on coastal sand dunes, however, there is the added challenge of coping with the exposed habitat, the instability of the sand and its high salt content, which comes from being so close to the sea. Only a select collection of plants and animals are adapted to survive in these harsh conditions. Finding these specialists thriving in their natural habitat is what makes a trek across the dunes so rewarding.

WILDLIFE WATCH

Where can I visit sand dunes?

Sand dunes are found all around the British coast, the largest and most abundant on the west coast. Most of the best dune systems are now partially or wholly within nature reserves. The rest are either privately owned or used for other purposes such as golf courses, but still retain considerable wildlife interest. You should always check that you are allowed to visit an area and keep to designated footpaths. Remember that dunes are easily damaged by repeated or careless trampling, which leads to serious wind erosion. Some reserves have solved the problem by laying out artificial walkways through the more vulnerable areas.

Dune areas that you can visit include:

● **Upton Towans, Cornwall**
A vast area of dunes centred at grid reference SW570395 but with many points of access. The South West Coast Path runs along the seaward side of the dunes.

● **Studland, Dorset**
Studland is a nature reserve at grid reference SZ034836 and has a dune nature trail.

● **Lytham St Annes, Lancashire**
This Lytham Council-maintained reserve is at grid reference SD309307.

● **Gibraltar Point, Lincolnshire**
A County Naturalists Trust reserve with marshes as well as dunes can be found at grid reference TF556581.

● **Blakeney Point, Norfolk**
This National Trust reserve is at grid reference TG015458.

● **Lindisfarne, Northumberland**
The dunes are one aspect of this national nature reserve at grid reference NU096432.

● **Kenfig Burrows, Glamorgan**
This superb area of dunes belonging to Bridgend County Borough Council is at grid reference SS802811.

● **Aberffraw Dunes, Anglesey**
A lovely area of dunes backing a popular beach is at grid reference SH357688.

● **Sands of Forvie, Aberdeenshire**
A large area of mixed coastal habitats, including dunes, is found at grid reference NK0227. Visitors must keep to the designated footpaths.

● **John Muir Country Park, East Lothian**
Estuary, beach and cliffs as well as dunes are in the area of grid reference NT6480.

● **Murlough National Nature Reserve, Co. Down**
Superb dunes – Ireland's first nature reserve – can be seen at grid reference J410350.

Birdlife on coastal cliffs

The noise may be deafening and the smell overpowering, but a visit to a well-established sea-bird colony during the breeding season is an unforgettable experience.

The Manx shearwater usually breeds on offshore islands and only returns to its nesting colony under cover of darkness, to avoid being attacked by gulls.

Sea birds are very particular about where they breed. Each type of bird has its own ideas about where it wants to nest and not just any old sheer face of rock or craggy pile will do.

To start with, cliffs need to be near rich feeding grounds. In this respect, the British Isles are fortuitously positioned at the point where the warm waters of the Atlantic Gulf Stream meet cold currents moving south from the Arctic Ocean. The battling currents stir up nutrients in the form of minute organisms that migrate to the surface. Here, these nutrients feed the microscopic plants and animals in the plankton and set the whole marine food cycle rolling; small fry are eaten by bigger fish which, in turn, become food for the sea birds.

Life on a ledge
The best breeding sites are found on sandstone or limestone cliffs where the hard sedimentary rock flakes away to form plenty of secure horizontal ledges. These are home to the biggest breeding colonies of sea birds.

Only a few hardy fulmars have colonised the crumbly gravel and sand cliffs of East Anglia, which are being washed away by the sea at an alarming rate – up to a metre of coastline disappears each year. Such rapid erosion creates cliffs that are rounded and slumped, without permanent ledges that can accommodate sea birds. At the other extreme, the toughest old volcanic (igneous) rocks, the granites, are solid masses that resist erosion and generally lack ledges for birds to settle on.

Likewise, the dazzling white cliffs of Sussex and Kent house few sea birds. Soft chalk crumbles too easily, so any ledges created may be unstable. In addition, any sea birds that used to breed there were put off long ago by people killing them for sport or stealing their eggs.

Not all sea birds opt for a precarious existence on the cliff face. The only gull to nest on ledges is the elegant kittiwake, which can balance its nest and eggs on the narrowest of rocky outcrops. Other species of gull, along with skuas and terns, favour flatter ground, either on the tops of cliffs or on remote or inaccessible coastal marshes and moorland.

Fish food
By and large, the populations of most cliff-nesting sea birds have fared quite well over the last century, although there are local exceptions. Chronic over-fishing of the seas around Britain has depleted numbers of bigger predatory fish and allowed the populations of smaller fish to thrive, which is good for the birds. In theory, sand-eels, which used to be eaten by larger fish species, should now be available for sea birds to eat. Unfortunately, in recent years sand-eel populations have crashed in some areas, too. This is due in part to industrial-scale fishing and the taking of fish for processing into fish meal, which is used as feed on fish farms or for livestock.

The popular puffin may look a little comical, but these plump, sturdy birds are superbly adapted to catching fish at sea.

Landing on a rocky outcrop is always a tricky challenge for a guillemot. It spends most of its time at sea, fishing.

Gannets nest in dense colonies. The space between neighbouring nests is determined by the pecking range of each bird.

From the moment they hatch, young kittiwakes display an impressive ability to remain firmly rooted to the spot. This is a vital skill, given the precarious position of their nest and the fatal consequences of a fall.

Cormorant colonies are among the smelliest of all sea-bird sites. The surrounding rocks and plants become drenched in a whitewash of bird droppings (guano). One plant, the tree mallow, can thrive in these conditions.

The best sea-bird cliffs offer a wide range of nooks and crannies for the birds, including rocky ledges, crevices, boulders and loose soil suitable for digging burrows.

SEA-BIRD POPULATIONS IN THE BRITISH ISLES

(as numbers of individuals)

European storm-petrel 320,000
Leach's storm-petrel 100,000
Manx shearwater 600,000
Fulmar 1,200,000
Gannet 450,000
Cormorant 24,000
Shag 92,000
Kittiwake 1,000,000
Guillemot 1,520,000
Razorbill 200,000
Black guillemot 40,000
Puffin 930,000

Sea birds are notoriously hard to count accurately. This applies particularly to the first three birds in the list, since they only return to their colonies after dark and nest in underground burrows. One of the auks, the razorbill, breeds in much smaller numbers than the guillemot: it is more difficult to census than its commoner relative as it likes to nest out of sight among thousands of guillemots lining the cliff ledges, in a cleft or among boulders. The other two auk species are also difficult to count, since the puffin nests in a burrow and the black guillemot under piles of boulders, but at least both are active by day.

Every bird in its place

When you watch a group of sea birds fishing, it becomes clear that they are exploiting different feeding opportunities according to their size, shape and behaviour. In a similar way, during the breeding season different sea birds nest in various locations on a cliff, which helps to avoid competition for sites. Not all cliffs offer suitable nesting places for every species of sea bird, but from looking at the type of coastline it is possible to make a good guess at which birds are most likely to breed there.

Sea cliffs provide a vertical set of nesting sites for birds, with a variety of locations up for grabs on the rock face. There is unlikely to be a natural cliff with quite as many nesting opportunities as the one illustrated on the left, but elements of it are recognisable on any sea-bird cliff. In the illustration, the birds are shown nesting in their favourite sites, but in reality they may have to make do with less than ideal positions.

At first glance, a large sea-bird colony looks absolutely chaotic. There are thousands of birds circling and darting about, squabbling over

ownership of a ledge and performing courtship, greeting and threat displays on the ledges and in the air. Yet as far as the birds are concerned, the best place to be is in the thick of it all, at the heart of the colony. The most experienced birds nest there and are the ones most likely to raise their young successfully.

High-rise neighbours

In a busy colony, no ledge or cleft large enough to hold an egg is left vacant. Heavy birds with relatively small wings, such as shags and cormorants, occupy lower sites. It is not worth them expending huge amounts of energy flying higher to breed farther up the cliff when there are vacant sites lower down. They cannot risk being too low down though, in case their nests or chicks are swept off the cliff by a freak wave in a summer storm. The ace fliers, the gannets and the fulmars, take the top bunks, high up on the cliff face or actually on the flat or gently sloping ground on the top.

Burrow-nesting shearwaters, petrels and puffins have very specific requirements. They hide their nests underground, so it is important that they find patches of soil that are easy to excavate. In the case of shearwaters and petrels in particular, they must be

● Herring gulls and lesser black-backed gulls favour grassy cliff tops for their nests

● Puffins excavate burrows in grassy slopes where soils are suitable

● Great black-backed gulls are solitary nesters on rocky outcrops

● Gannets or fulmars generally take the wide ledges

● Kittiwakes build nests and guillemots lay eggs directly on inaccessible and often narrow ledges

● Razorbills prefer rock crevices, caves and boulder slopes

● Shags usually nest low down on cliffs

● Black guillemots nest on boulder beaches

Parents and young use sound to help identify each other, so it may take some time for inbound birds to locate their nestlings above the general hullabaloo of the colony, and even longer to reach them through the wheeling mass of flying birds.

● Storm-petrels and shearwaters nest on offshore islands, where they may be joined by other sea birds

Where suitable rock ledges occur, guillemots often nest shoulder-to-shoulder causing problems for birds trying to come in to land.

CLIFF-NESTING BIRDS

Manx shearwater, European storm-petrel and Leach's storm-petrel
These are burrow-nesters, favouring grassy outcrops on cliffs or on the cliff top. All three species are rarely seen at the colony in daylight, but they have strange and distinctive calls that they make at night as they flock back into the colonies. These birds are long-distance migrants, and their colonies some of which may have 10,000 or more pairs – are remote and inaccessible. Petrels have a characteristic smell that may help them to find their nests in the final stages of navigation.
● **Breeding** Single large, white egg; incubation 6–7 weeks, fledging at around 9 weeks

Fulmar
The fulmar, a long-lived bird that may survive for 34 – and sometimes up to 50 – years, is present at the colony throughout the day. It is typically stiff-winged in flight. Frequently found nesting in nooks and crannies at the cliff top, it may even nest inland on rocky outcrops. Fulmar colonies are often quite loose and are still increasing after an amazing expansion in the bird's range and numbers over the last 120 years. Fulmars defend their nest sites by vomiting foul smelling oil at intruders.
● **Breeding** Single large, white egg incubated for 7–8 weeks; chick fledges after about 7 weeks; does not start breeding until it is 6–12 or more years old

Cormorant and shag
These big, black birds nest low down on the cliff or even on the flat tops of low offshore islands and rocky stacks. They sometimes get washed off by high tides and rough seas. They build nests and may steal nesting material from their neighbours. Shags are found in many areas, but cormorant colonies are few and far between. Cormorants feed by diving for fish; those feeding inland in the winter are considered pests by anglers.
● **Breeding** 3–4 eggs in a clutch – pale blue, becoming stained; incubation lasts just over 4 weeks, and fledging takes almost 5 weeks

Gannet
The largest British sea bird, the gannet nests on wide ledges and steep slopes on the tops of isolated islands. Gannet numbers have been increasing for many years. Tens of thousands may nest together in crowded colonies. Young birds have sooty brown feathers on their backs and wings that will eventually moult out to white before they start to breed at four years of age. The youngsters migrate southwards to North Africa and the Mediterranean for the winter, but the older birds stay closer to home. They feed by plunge diving.
● **Breeding** Single large, white egg incubated for 44 days, the chick leaves the nest about 13 weeks after hatching

Guillemot and razorbill
These two large auks crowd on to ledges in dense colonies. The guillemots nest closer together than any other bird – up to 20 or more pairs per square metre (two per sq ft). Razorbill nests are usually concealed under boulders in areas where guillemots are nesting on the ledges. Colonies often total many thousands. The birds may feed tens of kilometres from the nesting colony – they dive for fish and use their wings to propel their bodies under the water in pursuit of their prey.
● **Breeding** Single egg, generally blue or green, marked with a variable array of blotches, dots and scribbles; razorbill's egg is oval, the guillemot's is pointed, which prevents it from rolling off the ledge; incubation lasts about 5 weeks; young jump off ledge at about a third of their adult weight – they swim under the watchful eye of their parents at about 3 weeks old

Puffin and black guillemot
These are the two auks that nest in burrows. Puffins are most likely to be at the top of the cliff using burrows in the turf that they have made themselves or stolen from rabbits. Puffin colonies are dense and often very big, with the birds feeding over a wide area. Black guillemots, also known as tysties, usually favour boulder tumbles, just above the beach. Tysties have scattered small colonies and feed close to the nesting burrow. Like other auks, both feed on small fish.
● **Breeding** Single white egg for the puffin, 1 or 2 for the black guillemot; incubation 39 days for the puffin, slightly less for the tystie; fledging at 5–6 weeks

Throughout the breeding season, shags engage in bill and head-rubbing displays. These are most intense when courtship commences.

inaccessible to ground predators. Like puffins, black guillemots breed in burrows, but theirs are excavated between the boulders on the beach, just above the high watermark.

On the shelf
Guillemots choose flat or inward sloping ledges for nesting. They do not build a nest, so their unprotected eggs would roll off otherwise. Kittiwakes have no such worries, as they build secure nests that hold their eggs safely. Razorbills, on the other hand, use backward sloping ledges, preferably with some stones among which they can partly conceal their nests.

All sea birds are busy nesting from April to July. After that some species leave with their young for the open sea. Others, such as the fulmar and gannet, have chicks in open nests until late August or September. Burrow-nesting species, especially the petrels, may stay on the cliffs even longer. Many sea birds hang around the colonies outside the breeding season and defend their prized central nesting sites for months before the time comes for them to breed again.

Cliffs are also home to birds of prey, such as peregrines and kestrels. Ravens stick to wild, rocky coasts, nesting under cliff overhangs. Another crow, the chough with its red beak,

is rare, but a few still nest on craggy cliffs in west Wales. Rock doves, ancestors of the town pigeon, are cliff-ledge nesters. House martins may plaster their mud-cup nests to cliff faces and sand martins excavate their nesting tunnels in sand and gravel cliffs.

Razorbills often sit around on rocks in the vicinity of their nest sites, sometimes in the company of other auk species.

Visiting sea-bird colonies

Sea-bird colonies are scattered on cliffs all round our coasts, but the biggest and best are found in the north and west. The south and south-east coasts have the fewest colonies because there are fewer cliffs and the water off these coasts may be more polluted.

Colonies of sea birds usually gather in remote areas that are hard to reach. Some are on uninhabited islands that are rarely, if ever, visited by people; one or two of these are so magnificent they are included in the list opposite, even though they are almost impossible to reach. However, most of the colonies mentioned are reasonably accessible. Remember that many sea birds fledge in July, so the best dates to visit are between June and mid-July.

Steep cliffs are dangerous places unless you take great care. Always keep to the paths and follow any advice given to you in an information leaflet or by a warden. Often the edges of the cliffs are crumbly and may collapse if you venture too close. All birds are easily scared and may lose their eggs or young if you alarm them. On a calm day, one of the safest ways of watching sea birds nesting is to take an organised boat trip out to the colony.

◄ A gannet soars over the cliffs at Flamborough Head on long, narrow, wings with a span of up to 1.92m (6ft 4in). When it dives for fish, its wings close before it hits the water.

▲ The cliffs of Hermaness are about as far-flung as you can get in the British Isles. They are situated at the northern end of Unst in the Shetland Isles.

▼ From May to August each year, thousands of pairs of gannets are in residence on the craggy cliffs of the tiny island of Ailsa Craig in the Firth of Clyde.

▲ Situated on the east coast of Yorkshire, the mighty chalk cliffs of Flamborough Head have the largest mainland colony of gannets in Britain.

◄ Puffins breed at Flamborough Head, too. The size of fish that a parent puffin catches increases as its chick grows.

WILDLIFE WATCH

Where should I go to see sea-bird colonies?

◄ A large fulmar looks far more comfortable soaring over the cliffs or skimming above the open sea than it does coming in to land at its nest on the cliff top.

▲ Sea-bird colonies are found all around Britain's long and varied coastline. Some of the finest sites are marked on this map and detailed below.

◄ The Farne Islands are among the most accessible of all British sea-bird colonies. Large numbers of auks, gulls, terns and shags breed there every summer.

1 Bempton and Flamborough
These easily accessible hard chalk cliffs are the site of England's only gannet colony, founded about 30 years ago and now with over 1000 pairs. Other major species include kittiwakes, guillemots and razorbills. Guillemot eggs were once taken by local people for food.

2 Farne Islands
The small cliffs of these offshore islands support large numbers of sea birds, including gulls, terns and eider ducks. The islands are run by the National Trust. Licensed boatmen run trips from Seahouses on the Northumbrian coast. Inner Farne Island also has extensive archaeological remains.

3 St Abb's Head
A picturesque headland easily reached by public roads, St Abb's Head houses a varied breeding colony: the main occupants are guillemots and kittiwakes. The birds fly over the road to bathe in a freshwater loch behind the cliffs, putting on a noisy display for birdwatchers.

4 Bass Rock
A splendid colony of 60,000 gannets breeds on the rock, along with other birds. The gannets inhabit the sides of the island and the flat areas on top of it. Boat trips run from North Berwick. Alternatively, birds are visible from the mainland through binoculars.

5 Bullers of Buchan and Fowlsheugh
The Bullers of Buchan and Fowlsheugh are accessible mainland mixed colonies. In fact, there is a bus stop within 250 metres (273yd). More than 100,000 breeding birds feed offshore in the area that used to be fished from the ports of Peterhead, Aberdeen and Stonehaven.

6 Fair Isle
This famous bird observatory is a very important sea-bird colony. Kittiwakes, fulmars, shags, gannets and all the auks breed here in large numbers. The bird observatory is open to day visitors and there are crofts on the island that take guests. Access is by air or ferry from Shetland.

7 Hermaness
Shetland is one of the best places in the country to watch sea birds. The cliffs are home to huge numbers of birds, but remote islands such as Foula are difficult to reach. Hermaness, the northernmost headland on the island of Unst, has a huge gannet colony and just about every other species of breeding sea bird is present.

8 St Kilda
These extremely remote islands are very difficult to visit – even landing on some of the islands is so hazardous it is rarely attempted. St Kilda has the world's largest gannetry with more than 60,000 pairs, as well as in excess of 100,000 pairs of puffins and huge colonies of fulmars and kittiwakes.

9 Ailsa Craig
Gannets are the chief claim to fame of this great, uninhabited rock in the entrance to the Firth of Clyde, with 25,000 breeding pairs. Other sea-bird numbers may increase during the next few years, as rats have recently been eradicated.

10 Bardsey Island (Ynys Enlli)
This small trust-owned island off the tip of the Llŷn Peninsula in north Wales has a thriving Manx shearwater colony. Day trips and short stays are available.

11 Grassholm, Skokholm and Skomer
About 2km (1¼ miles) off the Marloes Peninsula in Dyfed lie several sea-bird islands. Huge Manx shearwater colonies on Skokholm and Skomer can be visited, but access to Grassholm, home to over 30,000 pairs of gannets, is trickier. A huge puffin colony was lost when their burrows undermined the turf so much that the topsoil was blown away.

12 Lundy
There are now only a handful of puffins nesting on Lundy, but colonies of shags, kittiwakes, guillemots and razorbills may be readily seen from the boat trips that are run from the Devon mainland.

13 Isles of Scilly
The Isles of Scilly have few significant cliffs – none is more than 30m (100ft) high – but many sea birds, common terns and puffins among them, have established small colonies. Boat trips are available for visitors.

The black guillemot is thinly distributed around the rocky headlands of the northern coasts.

Channel Islands – a cosmopolitan mix

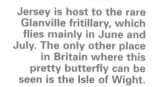

Thanks largely to the location of these islands, many unusual plants and animals from around the world have been successfully introduced over the years, making the region a naturalist's paradise.

Jersey is host to the rare Glanville fritillary, which flies mainly in June and July. The only other place in Britain where this pretty butterfly can be seen is the Isle of Wight.

At the mouth of the English Channel and the Gulf of St Malo lie the Channel Islands. Although this rocky cluster of islands is British, they are much closer to the coast of north-western France than to southern England. The largest of the islands, Jersey and Guernsey, are the main destinations for holiday-makers, but the smaller islands of Alderney and Sark get their fair share of visitors. There are numerous small islands and islets. Some, such as the Casquets, are little more than rocky outcrops that are a notorious danger to shipping. Others are little gems; a beach on Herm, a small private island between Guernsey and Sark, is popular with shell collectors, for instance. Most shell enthusiasts visit this molluscs' graveyard at least once in a lifetime. Among the hundreds of attractive and unusual shells found there are the dog cockle, common wendletrap and keyhole limpet.

Beneficial climate

Tourism and agriculture are the mainstays of the Channel Islands' economy, thanks largely to the temperate climate. They lie farther south than the rest of Britain and are bathed by the warm waters of the Gulf Stream sweeping in from the Atlantic. As a result, the Channel Islands enjoy a mellow maritime climate with no great seasonal fluctuations in temperature. Snow and frosts are rare in winter, while cooling sea

◄ Hottentot fig was introduced from southern Africa. Although the flowers are pretty, it forms extensive carpets which squeeze out native coastal plants.

▼ Jersey cows are famous for their rich and creamy milk. For those grazing on Jersey, the island's lush pastures must take some of the credit.

breezes take the burn out of heatwaves in the summer. Compared with most parts of mainland Britain, the Channel Islands are extremely sunny. The long hours of sunshine and uniform temperatures guarantee an extended and relatively stable growing period for plants. This is apparent from the lush native flora and is exploited by farmers. The rich pastures make good grazing for two of

The most dramatic scenery on Jersey is to be found along the north coast. Steep cliffs plunge into the sea and are battered by the waves.

the islands' best known breeds of dairy cattle: Jersey and Guernsey cows still thrive on their respective islands and are also bred for export.

Before people settled on the Channel Islands, thousands of years ago, the landscape was probably dominated by deciduous woodland. Since settlement, the extent of the woodland has been drastically reduced. Pockets of trees are now confined mainly to north-facing slopes and steep valley sides. Trees were cleared from the level and sunny south-facing slopes to create land for cultivation. Today, those fields are used to grow everything from early blooming flowers to the finest new potatoes.

Despite the clearances, there are still many small

woods of conifers, native elms and introduced sycamores. Hedgerows act as windbreaks, sheltering the growing crops.

Rare beauty

For nature enthusiasts, the Channel Islands offer excellent opportunities to explore some beautiful countryside and a variety of unspoilt habitats. Although much of the wildlife is familiar to visitors from Britain, there are subtle differences between

the flora and fauna of the Channel Islands and the mainland. Given the location of the islands, it is to be expected that most of the more unusual plants and animals were or are based on the Continent. Many are rare on mainland Britain and some occur nowhere else in the British Isles.

The Channel Islands have some stunning and dramatic coastal scenery. In spring, the cliff tops look spectacularly

RARE MAMMALS

The Channel Islands are home to a few small mammals rarely, if ever, seen elsewhere in Britain. The only trouble is that these creatures are shy and nocturnal, and so difficult to see. Greater white-toothed shrews are found on Alderney, Guernsey and Herm, but nowhere else in the British Isles. Sark and Jersey have populations of the lesser white-toothed shrew; its only other

British home is on the Scilly Isles. The French equivalent of the common shrew, Millet's shrew, is present on Jersey, but was probably introduced to the island by humans. Perhaps the most interesting of all the rodents is the common vole, which lives on Guernsey and Alderney. Oddly, the only other place in the British Isles where common voles can be found is on Orkney.

▲ The Guernsey vole, the local common vole also found on Alderney, may be native to the islands as it is widespread on the nearby French mainland.

◄ Lesser white-toothed shrews may occasionally be seen foraging for insects among leaf litter in hedgerows and near the coast.

▶ On sunny days, green lizards scurry among coastal dunes and heathland in Jersey. April and May are the best months to look out for them.

◀ The loose-flowered orchid, also known as the Jersey orchid, grows on marshy ground and in wet meadows in Jersey and Guernsey.

▶ In late spring and early summer, rare exotic visitors such as this colourful bee-eater may turn up, blown from Spain on warm southerly breezes.

found along a few stretches of shore, notably on the west coast of Jersey at Les Quennevais and on Guernsey, at the north and west of the island. The dunes are home to some of the Channel Islands' most exclusive wild flowers, such as the sand crocus, dwarf pansy and sand quillwort.

Woodland scene
A good way to explore inland Guernsey and Jersey, especially on a hot summer's day, is to walk along the shady lanes, overhung by gnarled trees and tangled shrubs. In this lush jungle, it is often difficult to see where the hedgerows end and the woodland begins. The hedges form sheltered corridors for wildlife and are excellent places to look out for small mammals and birds.

Familiar native trees, including English oak, ash, beech, alder, silver birch and hazel used to dominate the local woodlands. They are still there but now share the land with introduced species such as the sycamore, probably the most common tree on the Channel Islands. Turkey oaks

and holm oaks, liquidambar and sugar maple are well established, too.

Walk along the lanes in spring and you should have little difficulty in recognising many familiar woodland plants, such as bluebells, primroses, lesser celandine, alexanders, lords-and-ladies and herb robert. Mosses,

liverworts and ferns flourish in the humid conditions. Hart's-tongue fern is one of the most widespread species of fern on the islands.

For birdwatchers, the woodlands are quite a home from home. Most of the songbirds you are likely to see are common in southern

colourful when they are carpeted with seaside flowers such as thrift and sea campion. Not far inland from the coast, there are areas of maritime heath and grassland, each harbouring its own community of plants and animals.

Typical heathland plants such as western gorse, ling, bell heather and bracken predominate, creating dense cover that is a haven for rare birds such as the Dartford warbler. This pugnacious little bird scolds intruders on its territory with its harsh calls. Rare butterflies such as the Glanville fritillary cohabit with more widespread species including graylings and small coppers. These are joined in the summer by migrant butterflies from southern Europe such as the painted lady and pale clouded yellow.

In marked contrast to the rugged appearance of much of the coastline, extensive undulating sand dunes are

On Herm beach, you may find the pearly shell of an abalone, known locally as a common ormer. This impressive mollusc is found nowhere else in the British Isles.

England. Favourites such as robins, dunnocks, wrens, blackbirds, great tits and blue tits are joined in spring by migrants such as the blackcap, and garden and willow warblers.

There are a few significant absentees. You will not come across any nuthatches on the Channel Islands. The common treecreeper is absent too, although the almost identical short-toed treecreeper is present. This treecreeper breeds in France and Spain but is not found anywhere else in the British Isles, unless it turns up as a rare visitor.

Many migrant birds follow coastal routes when flying between their breeding grounds and the countries where they overwinter. Even more make an unscheduled landing on the coast in rough weather. Given the position of the Channel Islands, it is almost inevitable that they are an important staging post for migrating birds in spring and autumn. Many of the common migrants, such as warblers and flycatchers, breed here rather than in mainland Britain. Rare sightings of Mediterranean species, such as bee-eaters and woodchat shrikes are a special treat.

Summer blooms

The most fabulous displays of coastal flowers occur from May to early July, although the peak of flowering varies from year to year depending on the weather. During the summer months, it is obvious how thrift, a favourite coastal plant, earned its alternative name of sea pink. Other species that are widespread on the coasts of southern England, such as sea campion, common scurvygrass, sea plantain, sea beet and sea spurrey, grow alongside it.

A closer look may reveal more unusual and localised plants such as the prostrate

The boldly marked shrikes are handsome birds but their heavy, hooked black beaks and the black mask across their eyes make them look somewhat menacing. They hunt like miniature hawks, waiting on a prominent perch to ambush their prey. As soon as an insect scuttles into view, the shrike pounces on it.

They also eat lizards, small rodents and birds.

Most shrikes spend the winter in Africa but breed in Europe. The woodchat shrike breeds around the Mediterranean, but some overshoot and may end up as far north as the Channel Islands in late spring and early summer.

Distinguished by its chestnut cap and bold black and white plumage, a woodchat shrike watches for potential prey scurrying underneath its look-out perch.

The southern side of Jersey slopes gently towards the sea. Along the south coast, broad stretches of sandy beach, as here at Greve de Lecq, become playgrounds for holiday-makers in the summer.

▼ The flowers of sand crocus appear in early spring, when they look like tiny jewels studding a few areas of coastal turf in the Channel Islands.

► As its name suggests, the Jersey buttercup grows nowhere else in Britain. The large, glossy flowers appear in May, but they soon die back.

► To see the short-toed treecreeper in Britain, you have to travel to the Channel Islands. Otherwise you would find it in woodland on mainland Europe.

form of broom or the spotted rock-rose, found mainly around the Mediterranean. Later in the season, the nationally scarce autumn squill puts on fine displays in short turf on many cliff tops.

The Channel Islands have an impressive number of native plants – Guernsey alone is home to about a thousand different species. Over the years, the list of naturally occurring flowers has been added to considerably by zealous botanists and keen gardeners. In some cases, this is a result of deliberate planting, but most of the interlopers are garden species that have escaped into the wild. Several of these plants are colourful, but not all are entirely welcome additions to the local flora because they have a way of taking over and crowding out the local plants.

Flamboyant foreigners

Outside the confines of parks and gardens where alien species are cultivated, keep an eye out for stunning displays of hottentot fig. Carpets of its bright pink flowers are hard to miss along the cliff tops from May to July. This impressive plant hails from South Africa but is now naturalised on the islands. Elsewhere on the coast, clumps of Duke-of-Argyll's teaplant liven up the scenery, and the brightly coloured Bermuda buttercup may be found in abundance along sheltered field edges.

It is this blend of native plants and animals living alongside exotic newcomers and unexpected visitors that makes a trip to the Channel Islands such a voyage of discovery for naturalists and gardeners.

▼ Guernsey is famous for its cliff paths and the Water Lanes. Each picturesque, shady lane follows its own stream down to a bay.

Places to visit in the Channel Islands

Easily reached by ship or plane, the Channel Islands are popular destinations for British holiday-makers. The attractions are obvious – blue skies, inviting seas and stunning coastal scenery. For wildlife enthusiasts, the islands never fail to live up to expectations.

Miles 0   5   10   15
Km 0   5   10   15   20   25   30

1 Jersey
The largest of the Channel Islands, Jersey is an island of contrasts. The north coast is bounded by dramatic rocky cliffs and the south by gently shelving sands. Coastal heathland is found all around the island, but by far the most extensive area is at Les Landes in the north-western corner. The richest wildlife site is Les Quennevais, where the extensive sand dunes are colonised by sand crocus, dwarf pansy and sand quillwort, and green lizards may be seen basking in the sun or scuttling across the sand.

2 Guernsey
Guernsey has some stunning coastal scenery, which is most rugged along the southern coast. A footpath enables visitors to experience a wonderful array of coastal flowers in spring. The maritime heath is home to linnets, stonechats and Dartford warblers, as well as green lizards. Other places to visit include the Silbe Nature Reserve, which harbours loose-flowered orchids along with many other marshland species, Pleinmont Point and L'Ancresse Common, an area of sand dunes.

3 Alderney
The breathtaking coastal scenery makes this small island well worth a visit. The south cliffs are rich in wild flowers, such as prostrate broom. There are carpets of thrift and patches of western gorse, kidney-vetch and bird's-foot trefoil. Numerous sea birds breed on the cliffs, notably at Giffoine Point, and on offshore islands. In low-lying areas, look out for the sand crocus in spring, and autumn squill and autumn lady's-tresses later on in the year.

4 Sark
Best known for its sheer cliffs and a huge variety of wild flowers, Sark is a small windswept granite plateau that rises abruptly from the sea. Apart from its maritime flora, which include the rare sand crocus, the island is a refuge for considerable numbers of migrant songbirds, grounded during spring and autumn storms.

5 Herm
The tiny island of Herm has some imposing cliffs at its southern end, where sea birds, such as puffins, nest. It is best known for its shell beach and the dunes composed of shell sand that dominate its northern half.

Lavender is cultivated at St Brelade on Jersey, for the perfume industry. Fields of this fragrant Mediterranean herb turn the landscape purple.

Animals and plants in focus

Waterside watch

- The otter – back from the brink
- The water shrew
- Dazzling kingfisher
- Recognising surface-feeding ducks
- The grass snake
- The edible frog
- Recognising dragonflies
- Swarms of midges
- Water-crowfoots: floating carpets

The otter – back from the brink

With its supple body, thick fur and webbed paws, the otter is suited to life in water and on land. Once on the verge of disappearing from England altogether, it is gradually returning to our rivers and shores. Western Scotland now has one of the biggest otter populations in Europe.

In the wild, otters are charming, playful animals, a joy to watch as they frolic among seaweed and rocks – but very few people have ever seen a wild otter. The good news is that there are probably more otters around than you might think. They are fairly widespread along remote stretches of Scottish coastline, in sea lochs and estuaries. The otter is gradually becoming more numerous in Wales and south-west England. Unfortunately, otters disappeared from much of central and eastern England in the mid-1950s, largely due to the destruction of their habitat and pollution caused by pesticides. They are staging a comeback but their recovery is slow. Reports of otters on the upper

The sleek, handsome otter is still nowhere near as widespread or common in England or Wales as it once was.

reaches of the River Thames, as far east as Shiplake, just south of Henley, are cause for optimism.

Following the clues

As you walk along a river bank or seashore in an area where you might expect to find otters, look out for their droppings and signs of their tracks in the mud or soft sand. Their footprints are 6–7cm (2½–2¾in) long and show five toes, although the fifth toe is not always clear. Dog and fox prints have only four toes. Fresh tracks often show the marks of the webbing between the toes and claws too.

Another telltale sign is a well-used muddy chute worn through the vegetation down a steep bank into the water. No other animal is likely to create

Seeing an otter is a rare treat, especially during the day. If you move quietly through an area known to be an otter's haunt, you may glimpse one resting at the water's edge or sleeping on a rock.

Otters rely mainly on touch and smell for catching prey. The prominent whiskers are vital sensory organs, especially at night or in murky water. The forward-facing eyes suggest that they have good binocular vision in daylight.

A safe retreat

The otter frequents rivers, lakes and seashores. A solitary animal mainly active at night (except in parts of north-west Scotland and Shetland), it needs secluded lying-up places where it can rest in the day. An otter may have up to 30 different lairs around its territory – all within about 50m (165ft) of the water's edge – so that, after a night's hunting, it never has far to go to find a safe resting place. It often builds daytime underground dens, called holts, among riverside tree roots; sometimes it makes a couch from grass and twigs as an above-ground den, known as a hover. In fine weather an otter may sleep out in the open among the rocks on the shore or river bank.

OTTER FACT FILE

The otter is a member of the weasel family, which makes it a close relative of the stoat, polecat and pine marten. It has the same long, lithe body and short legs, and often runs with an arched back. But there the similarities end; the otter is much heavier and larger and spends much of its time in water.

● **NAMES**
Common name: otter
Scientific name: *Lutra lutra*

● **HABITAT**
Rivers, lakes and sheltered coastal areas

● **DISTRIBUTION**
Rare or absent from much of central and south-east England; small stronghold in East Anglia; widespread in south-west England, Wales, north of England, Scotland and Ireland

● **STATUS**
Probably 7000–10,000, of which most live in Scotland

● **SIZE**
Male length up to 90–130cm (35½–51¼in), of which about 35–45cm (14–17¾in) is tail; weight 6–15kg (14–33lb); female slightly smaller

● **VOICE**
Short, shrill whistle is most common; brief exchanges of chirping between adults and cubs; sometimes growls, chatters or hisses

● **FOOD**
Mainly fish; also crustaceans, molluscs, insects, worms, frogs; sometimes birds and small mammals

● **BREEDING**
Any time, but most births May–August, especially in Shetland; normally 2 or 3 cubs in a litter

● **NEST**
May use up to 30 lairs for daytime shelter; for breeding, a den is built above flood level

● **YOUNG**
Born after 62 days gestation, measuring about 12cm (4½in) in length and weighing about 100g (3½oz); cubs swim at 3 months and leave home at around 10–12 months

PROTECTED!

The otter is afforded full legal protection under Schedule 5 of the Wildlife and Countryside Act. It is an offence to kill otters or disturb them or their nests.

Many otters live along the rocky coasts of Scotland and the Western Isles. Here they can often be seen in broad daylight, catching crabs and rock-pool fish among the seaweed-draped boulders along the shore.

Distribution map key

■	Present
□	Not present, or rare

The external ears are quite small, but hearing is acute.

The fur is very dense – the underfur alone can have up to 70,000 hairs per cm² (over 450,000 hairs per sq in).

The webbed feet and the rudder-like tail are well-adapted for swimming.

OTTER-SPOTTING

Watching otters requires great patience. Finding signs that there is an otter about is much easier than catching sight of one. The clues are surprisingly obvious once you know what to look for. Otter droppings, called spraints, are the most common sign. These are smeared as territorial scent markers on rocks and logs above the water level in rivers, at the edge of lakes and under bridges. The spraints are small, 6–8cm (2½–3¼in) long and 1cm (½in) in diameter. You may see little clusters, with some spraints fresher than others. Recent ones look sticky and very black, like a patch of thick crude oil; older, drier ones are grey and powdery, like ash

Look out for tar-like droppings on rocks and tree trunks beside rivers and on quiet beaches – they are a sure sign that an otter has been in the area recently.

on a burnt-away cigarette. Closer inspection reveals fragments of prey – fish bones, scales and bits of crayfish or crab shells. The only other droppings likely to be seen along the water's edge that resemble otter spraints are those of the mink. These are black, about 6cm (2½in) long, with a twisted tip, and contain bones and shells too. However, otter spraints have a curious oily smell, which is surprisingly sweet; mink droppings smell acrid in comparison. If you find evidence of an otter, sit quietly out of sight and wait since the creature may pass that way again.

such a slide. Where slow-moving rivers meander through grassy fields, an otter may take a regular short cut across a bend, leaving a well-worn trail from one bank to the next. Occasionally, you may come across a partially eaten fish that could be the remains of an otter's meal, although it could have been left behind by other animals, too.

An otter can travel over 10km (6 miles) in a night and males visit up to 80km (50 miles) of river in a year. Normally one otter occupies a 10–15km (6–9 mile) stretch of river bank or lake side. Coastal otters usually have smaller territories, perhaps as little as 2km (1¼ miles) of shoreline. This may be because food is more abundant by the sea and rock-pool fish, such as blennies, butterfish and gobies, are easier to catch than bigger river fish. Mountain streams and lakes often have very few fish and otters are thinly dispersed in these areas.

Swimming and diving

Otters are adapted for an amphibious way of life, in which they rest and breed on land but catch most of their food in water. An otter is very agile in the water: when it dives its lithe body can twist and turn, changing direction swiftly. When swimming at the surface, the otter often

Explore quiet river banks for signs of otter activity.

Otters often prefer to hunt in streams and tributaries rather than in large rivers, because fish and other prey are easier to catch in shallow water.

Sensitive nose

Otters have an acute sense of smell which they use to locate their prey, to find each other and to detect danger.

Before retiring to its den to rest, an otter warily checks that it's safe to do so by taking a good sniff of the area, tentatively raising its head and twitching its long whiskers.

If the air confirms that the coast is clear, the otter lifts its head and takes one last careful look around before entering its den.

OTTER HUNTING

Until quite recently, otter hunting was a traditional rural pursuit. It was most popular in the 1930s, when about 400 otters were killed every year. Even as recently as the 1950s, there were a dozen active otter hunts. Each operated for 40–50 days every year, killing an average of 200 otters between them.

The hunters formed a line across a small river and, armed with long poles, walked slowly upstream, thrashing the water and forming a barrier to prevent the otter from doubling back. Otter hounds would forge ahead, seeking the scent and signs of otters in burrows and under tree roots along the banks.

When a find was made, the chase could last for an hour or more. Sometimes the otter got away, but often it did not. This beautiful animal was hunted mainly for sport although its reputation for being a nuisance to anglers, and salmon fishermen in particular, was often used to justify the culls.

When a wet otter comes ashore, it shakes vigorously and rolls about in the grass to dry its fur quickly. If it hears anything alarming, it may sit up on its haunches, supported by its tail, to take a good look around.

Otters rarely stay underwater for more than 30–40 seconds. If forced to remain submerged for more than couple of minutes without taking a breath, they might drown.

creates a distinctive V-shaped wake extending from its muzzle.

The otter's fur is very dense, trapping air close to the skin, which helps to keep it warm, even in freezing cold water. As an otter dives smoothly out of sight, the pressure of the water squeezes some of this air out of the fur, leaving a giveaway trail of bubbles rising to the surface. Loss of some of the insulating layer of air causes a drop in body temperature and is one reason why otters normally dive in shallow water where the water pressure is low, so less air is forced out. On the other hand, the air in the fur also acts like an unwanted life jacket, making the otter more buoyant, so it has to work harder to stay submerged. This energetic paddling means that an otter soon gets out of breath and needs to surface to take a gulp of air. After swimming in sea water otters like to bathe in freshwater pools to rinse the salt from their fur and keep each hair clean and separate.

Hunting and feeding

Otters are skilled predators and feed on a wide variety of prey, including fish, frogs and crustaceans, which they catch in the water. Occasionally, they also catch mammals, such as rats and water voles, and some birds. Their hunting behaviour is very adaptable and they take advantage of whatever feeding opportunities arise. They grope in muddy water to find fish among tree roots, nuzzle submerged stones to catch crayfish hiding underneath and even seize moorhens sitting on their nests.

Most of the otter's diet consists of fish. An adult otter needs to eat about 20 per cent of its body weight in food every day. Normally, in shallow water, an otter chases its prey this way and that until the fish tires, then snatches it in its teeth. Shallow pools are best because the fish cannot get away easily and the otter can surface quickly and regularly to breathe. In deeper water, an otter approaches its prey from below, so the fish cannot see it coming. Many dives end unsuccessfully; in water more than 2m (6½ft) deep, the otter may take as many as 12 attempts to catch anything. In shallow rock pools, it may be successful in a third of its dives, but then the prey, such as a blenny, is generally small and weighs only around 100g (3½oz). In lakes, the fish tend to be larger: an otter often takes eels weighing

On fine days, an otter likes to rest out in the open and bask in the sunshine. It is almost impossible to catch it unawares; at the first hint of intruders, it slips quietly into the nearby water and disappears.

An otter's fur is thick enough to keep it warm and dry when it swims in freezing cold water. Even so, an otter usually spends no more than 20–30 minutes in the water before coming ashore to dry off.

up to 500g (1lb 2oz). It only needs to catch about three fish of that size to satisfy its hunger for a whole day.

Family life

Otters usually live alone, unless the female is rearing a family of cubs. Adults rarely meet in the wild: when two rival males encounter one another, a fight may ensue. Fighting involves plenty of squealing and chasing, even some biting, until one of them concedes and runs away. The male and female only meet up to mate, attracted to each other when the female is fertile by a combination of scent and whistling. As a prelude to mating, there is often a period of courtship, when a male and female indulge in some energetic, flirtatious chases, romping about on land or in the water. They then

mate, either on land or while swimming; coupling can take up to half an hour. Afterwards, the two animals separate and return to their solitary lives. The male plays no part in raising the cubs.

Otters can breed at any time of the year, probably because British winters are relatively mild and food is never scarce. Most cubs are born between May and August. Females can bear a litter every year, but nearly half of them probably

raise a family every other year. Gestation lasts about 62 days. During this time, the female otter digs an underground breeding den, known as a holt. She may select somewhere well away from water or along a small tributary rather than beside a big river. The site is always above the level likely to be reached by flood waters. She lines the holt with dry grass and moss to make a cosy chamber in which she gives birth to her cubs. Usually there are two or three in a litter, although occasionally as many as five are born.

At birth, otter cubs are pink with a thin fuzz of pale fur. They measure about 12cm (4⅛in) in length and weigh just 100g (3½oz). For the first four or five weeks of their lives, the cubs are blind and utterly helpless. They are totally dependent on their mother for warmth and milk, suckling frequently and making little chirruping noises.

The cubs grow slowly, and at four or five weeks weigh about 700g (1lb 9oz). They start eating solid food when they are roughly seven weeks old, by which time their weight has increased to about 1kg (2lb 4oz). In another three weeks they venture outside the holt to play. The cubs eventually leave home when they are

OTTER OR MINK?

The otter is often mistaken for the American mink, introduced into this country for the fur trade and now well established in the wild.

● Compared with a cat, the otter is noticeably larger and the mink smaller.

● The otter is a milk-chocolate colour, darker when wet; a mink's coat is usually dark brown all over, apart from a little white on the chin.

● The otter has a flat, broad head with prominent whiskers; the mink has a pointed muzzle.

● An otter's tail is long, cylindrical and tapered; the mink's is bushy, when dry.

● The otter is shy and rarely seen in daylight; the mink is bold and often seen during the day.

The otter's throat and belly are paler than its back – an easy way to distinguish it from a mink.

At low tide the rocks are a playground where young otters romp in the slippery brown seaweed called kelp. When the tide comes in, the otters go hunting for the fish and crabs that live there.

A definite chute in the snow like this is a very good sign that an otter, or maybe even a family of otters, has been in the area lately.

Growing up

Otter cubs develop a waterproof coat by the time they are two or three months old. Soon after, they start having swimming and hunting lessons from their mother. At first, some cubs are reluctant to take the plunge and may need a push.

After a successful fishing expedition, the cubs re-scent each other by rubbing against the base of their mother's tail and spreading her scent over each other's fur. Tired out, they then curl up and fall asleep.

Young otters are extremely playful creatures and spend a lot of time clambering over their mother or rolling about the river bank engaged in mock fights.

10–12 months old. The average number of young otters reared to independence is less than two per female per year, but the success rate may be higher in years when food is abundant.

The first few weeks out on its own are a testing time for a young otter. It has to get used to catching all its own food and find shelter during the day as well as seek out and establish a new territory for itself. Inevitably this means travelling some way from its mother's home area. Many young otters die at this stage, either through malnutrition or from being run over as they cross roads looking for a suitable place to live. Fewer than half the cubs live to see their fourth birthday, but those that do survive their first two or three years have a reasonable chance of living for six or seven years. Perhaps one otter in a hundred reaches ten years of age.

The main threats to all otters are a shortage of food and the ever-present risk of being run over. Oil spills are another hazard for those living in coastal waters, especially around Shetland. Some

get caught up and drown in eel traps. In the past, many were killed or rendered infertile by pesticides. Pesticides are less of a problem nowadays, but eating fish contaminated by chemical spills and effluents may become a real threat as otters begin to recolonise rivers in industrial areas, such as the Midlands.

Rosy future

The positive news is that many river authorities are now spending significant amounts of money on improving the water quality and fish stocks of their rivers. Some are also providing lying-up places where otters can rest during the day. Such measures will surely help otter numbers recover from an all-time low in the 1960s and 1970s. Already there are more otters living in Britain than in almost any other country in Europe.

WILDLIFE WATCH

Where can I see otters?

● Otters are extremely shy and usually nocturnal. However, coastal otters are often active in the daytime. The best places to see otters are in Shetland and western Scotland, including the Hebridean islands, especially along quiet rocky shores and around sea lochs.

● There is an otter haven and visitors' hide at the southern end of the Isle of Skye, and otters are frequently seen on Loch Sunart and the Isle of Mull.

● The RSPB reserve at Leighton Moss in Lancashire has hides from which otters are quite often seen.

● If you locate a sprainting spot by a bridge over a river in Wales, Devon or the north of England, it is well worth spending an hour or two watching for the otter from the bridge at dawn or dusk.

● Otters are present on areas of low-lying wet fields, such as the Somerset Levels, but there are few vantage points from which to watch them and nowhere to hide.

● You can be certain of seeing otters in semi-natural surroundings at the Otter Trust, Earsham, near Bungay in Suffolk, or at other Trust sites including the Tamar Otter Sanctuary near Launceston in Cornwall, the North Pennines Reserve at Bowes near Barnard Castle in Co. Durham and the Norfolk Wildlife Park in Norwich. Telephone the Otter Trust's headquarters on 01986 893470 for details.

● Some zoos keep otters in pools where you may be able to see them swimming underwater.

The water shrew

This busy little animal, which must consume half its body weight in food each day, spends most of its short life on the move. A resident of streams and ditches, it may announce its presence with a shrill squeak.

To see one of these frenetic little creatures scurrying about the water's edge is a treat well worth the patience required. Clear chalk streams, watercress beds and unpolluted ditches or ponds are the places where the water shrew chooses to live. It needs to eat a large amount – half its body weight – every day, and so spends much of its time hunting in freshwater and in lush waterside vegetation.

The water shrew is perfectly adapted for this amphibious lifestyle. A ridge of stiff hairs stretches along the underside of its tail, effectively broadening it into a flat rudder that enables the shrew to steer underwater. The tiny toes on its hind feet are fringed with bristly hairs which give the feet some resistance to the water, allowing the shrew to swim more efficiently than if it had smooth toes. Underwater, it is the hind feet that provide most of the propulsion, enabling the water shrew to dive to depths of 70cm (28in) or more.

As the water shrew swims, the pressure of the water around it squeezes air from its fur, leaving a trail of tiny silvery bubbles. Some bubbles remain on the fur, and glisten like a silvery coating over its body. The air makes the shrew buoyant, so diving is hard work – if it stops paddling with its hind feet, it immediately bobs back to the surface like a cork. To stay submerged, the shrew may lodge itself temporarily against a small stone or grip on to some underwater vegetation while seeking out its prey.

Water shrews are reliant on freshwater for their food, but nevertheless they do stray some distance from streams and ponds. They have been found in woodlands, hedgerows and on chalk downland, up to a few miles from the nearest body of freshwater. They have also occasionally been reported living on coastal beaches in Scotland, where they probably feed on sandhoppers and other small seashore creatures among the boulders above the high watermark.

HAIR CARE

When it comes ashore after a dive, a water shrew shakes itself vigorously to get rid of the water in its coat. Then it scratches and licks its fur to comb out any matted hairs. To finish its grooming routine, the shrew squeezes down its burrow or between densely packed grass stems to smooth the fur and remove any specks of dust or debris that may be sticking to it.

It is essential that the water shrew cleans its fur well as it relies on its thick coat to keep it warm and dry under water. Air is trapped between the hairs, creating an insulating layer that stops the shrew from losing body heat in the cold water; and the fur is water repellent, which helps to prevent its skin from getting wet.

Sit beside a slow-flowing stream and you may be rewarded with a sighting of a water shrew, foraging busily but unobtrusively along the shallow margins.

WATER SHREW FACT FILE

Larger than other species of shrew, the water shrew is mainly nocturnal, emerging from its burrow just before dawn to forage. This mammal tends to stay fairly close to its burrow, which may be in a bank and have an underwater entrance.

● **NAMES**
Common name: water shrew
Scientific name: *Neomys fodiens*

● **HABITAT**
Streams and ponds, especially clear waters; woodlands and hedges, occasionally some distance from water; reported among boulders on Scottish beaches

● **DISTRIBUTION**
Patchy, but found throughout mainland Britain and also on some offshore islands

● **STATUS**
Estimated 1,900,000 individuals; least common of British mainland shrews

● **SIZE**
Length 6.5–9.5cm (2½–3¾in), tail 4.5–7.5cm (1¾–3in); weight 12–18g (¼–¾oz), but pregnant female about 10g (¼oz) heavier

● **FEATURES**
Velvety black fur above, and white, grey or yellowish below; small ears, often white tipped; tiny eyes; fringe of stiff hairs along underside of tail and also edging hind toes; small, red-tipped teeth

● **HABITS**
Active, scurries around in dense grass and lush, low vegetation; swims well and often; solitary except when mother is rearing young

● **VOICE**
Piercing squeak or rolling *churr* when alarmed, angry or excited

● **FOOD**
Large quantities of freshwater shrimps, aquatic insect larvae, small snails; also insects, worms and other invertebrates; occasionally small fish and young frogs

● **BREEDING**
Some females have first litter when 2–3 months old, but most breed in summer following birth; mating occurs April–June; usually 2 or 3 litters born per year, each with an average of 6 young

● **NEST**
Underground in tunnel system or beneath a log; woven from dry grass

● **YOUNG**
Born after 14–21 days gestation; leave nest at about 6 weeks old; young less distinctively marked than adult; fur brown above and dingy buff beneath

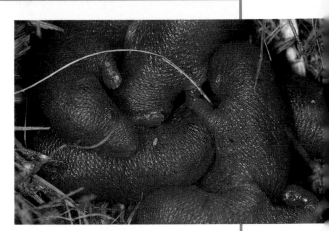

Naked, blind and helpless, new-born water shrews depend upon their mother for survival. Youngsters grow quickly and are usually weaned about a month after birth.

WATER SHREWS AND THE LAW

All shrews have a limited degree of protection under the Wildlife and Countryside Act, 1981. You are not allowed to trap water shrews without a licence.

Distribution map key

■ Present all year round

□ Not present

There is a sharp contrast between the dark upperparts and the white or pale underparts.

Tiny eyes suggest it hunts mainly by smell or touch.

The snout is slender, pointed and mobile.

Ear tips and eyebrows are often white.

A double row of stiff hairs forms a ridge along the tail.

The tail is about three-quarters of the body length.

There is a fringe of silvery white hairs on the hind feet.

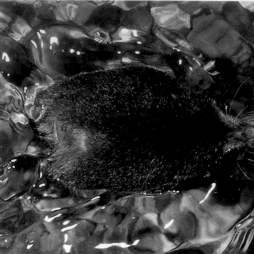

◄ In its endless quest for food, a water shrew tackles almost any very small animal it comes across. Crane flies are eagerly consumed as soon as they emerge in spring and early summer.

When swimming in a shallow stream, the water shrew looks sleek and shiny. At first glance or from a distance, it could be mistaken for a large water beetle.

Distribution

The water shrew is found all over mainland Britain, right to the north of Scotland, but there are large gaps in its coverage. In some cases, areas measuring tens of square miles have never had a reported sighting. The water shrew is found on many islands – including Anglesey, the Isle of Wight and various Scottish islands, such as Arran, Raasay, Skye, Mull and Bute – but not on the isles of Scilly, the Channel Islands or anywhere in Ireland.

It is unlikely that the water shrew reached these offshore islands without human assistance. At some time in the past, a shrew or two was probably scooped up with bundles of animal fodder or newly cut reeds intended for thatching or bedding, and accidentally transported to an island. This seems to have happened with many small mammal species.

The water shrew is far less abundant than either the common or pygmy shrew and lives at a lower density of population compared with other small mammals. Water shrews average three individuals per hectare in their most favoured habitat, watercress beds, where a maximum of about nine individuals per hectare has been recorded. This contrasts with densities of up to 100 common shrews in a typical hectare of grassland habitat, or wood mice in woodland.

Undigested remnants of water shrews turn up infrequently in owl pellets, which is a good indicator of the creature's rarity. They form just a tiny proportion of all the small mammals caught by barn owls (almost a third of barn owl captures may be common shrews). The water shrew is also seldom caught by cats or in small mammal traps. Its apparent scarcity is all the more surprising since it is about twice the size of the common shrew. This size advantage and its poisonous saliva mean that the water shrew can capture relatively large prey. It consumes small fish and frogs that the common shrew would be unable to tackle successfully, despite being notoriously ferocious.

The water shrew is easily recognised, so it is unlikely to be overlooked or confused with the common shrew, or any other small mammal. An adult water shrew is a very handsome creature. Typically, its back is a sleek, glossy black, and it has a sharply contrasting white belly, which is

Underwater exploration

The water shrew spends much of its time hunting for prey in water. It dives in the shallows of ponds and streams for prolonged periods, although it does have to return to the surface frequently to breathe.

When diving, the water shrew paddles furiously with both its front and hind legs to avoid bobbing back up to the surface.

The water shrew's sensitive mobile whiskers are probably a vital tool in its search for underwater prey.

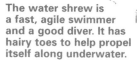

The water shrew is a fast, agile swimmer and a good diver. It has hairy toes to help propel itself along underwater.

Underwater, tiny air bubbles trapped in the water shrew's fur give it a silvery appearance. This sometimes makes a shrew visible in a clear stream.

Its hairy toes splayed for swimming, the water shrew powers its way back to the surface of the water to take a breath. The air trapped in its fur makes it buoyant.

often yellowish towards the middle. White cyebrows and car tips arc frequently visible. The tail is dark on top and whitish below. There is a good deal of variation within this pattern, and all-black individuals are more common in this species than in other shrews.

Dietary habits

The water shrew is active all year round, but harsh winters take their toll. When water around the edges of streams and ponds freezes solid for days or even weeks, the shrew is prevented from diving for food, and starvation becomes a real threat. Shrews usually catch half their food on the stream bed.

Water slaters, freshwater shrimps, small snails and the aquatic larvae of insects, such as caddis flies and damselflies, are the shrew's underwater prey. Their small, red-tipped teeth arc sharp and well adapted for seizing and chewing up active

If a potential meal is detected hiding beneath stones on the stream bed, the shrew digs away debris to reach it.

Having captured its quarry, the water shrew surfaces and returns to the bank or a rock by the stream to eat it.

VENOMOUS BITE

The water shrew is able to kill surprisingly large animals, such as newts, frogs and small fish. Studies have shown that it has a poisonous component in its saliva with which it paralyses its prey.

The water shrew usually bites its victims behind the head with its sharp little teeth. The poisonous saliva enters the prey's bloodstream through the wound and circulates to the brain, nerves and muscles, stopping the victim from struggling. The poison comes from the shrew's normal saliva-producing glands under the tongue. It is not very powerful, and bites to humans are not dangerous, even if the skin is punctured. Sometimes a reddish inflammation persists for a while, but there are no other ill effects.

Having mildly toxic saliva enables the water shrew to capture fish as big as a bullhead. Sometimes the remains of partially eaten snails, amphibians and fish are hoarded to be finished later.

Standing on its hind feet, snout raised, the water shrew sniffs for odours carried on the breeze. If it detects another water shrew, it may call out in shrill squeaks.

prey including brittle-shelled crustaceans, molluscs and insects. The iron deposits in the enamel of the red tips probably increase their resistance to wear.

The water shrew thrusts its long snout under pebbles and into tangles of vegetation in search of food. In dark water, its hunt is aided by long, sensitive whiskers on its snout. Larger prey is often brought ashore to favoured feeding sites on the banks or rocks nearby. Keen-eyed observers may notice telltale piles of remains, such as caddis-fly cases and snail shells, at the water's edge.

Unsurprisingly, the water shrew's black droppings contain the remains of such aquatic prey. With the help of a microscope or a powerful magnifying glass, it is possible to identify the finely chewed fragments and distinguish them from the droppings of common shrews.

Territorial instinct

Water shrews live in small burrows, about 2cm (¾in) in diameter. They sometimes adopt tunnels dug by moles and bank voles. The network of burrows includes small nesting chambers, in which dry grass and sometimes leaves are gathered to form bedding. Here, the resident shrew may spend several hours a day asleep. It also probably takes naps elsewhere in its burrow system or in the runways it has forged through the surrounding vegetation.

Little is known about the everyday life of the water shrew, apart from the fact that it is mainly active under cover of darkness – although occasionally a shrew may be seen foraging for brief periods during the day. Water shrews often live in close proximity to one another, but they are solitary creatures and each individual

keeps to itself, with adjacent home ranges overlapping very little.

Water shrews do not range widely, usually travelling no farther than 50m (55yd) from their nests. Home territories are small, perhaps 20–50m² (215–540sq ft) of land, with a similar area of water. Their well-developed scent glands and behaviour in captivity suggest that they are territorial animals. They mark out their ranges with small piles of droppings left on top of logs or stones to warn off intruders.

During the summer, water shrews may move about more, sometimes making excursions of up to 200m (220yd). Occasionally, they simply pack up and move to another location entirely. Individuals forced to move when streams dry up in summer might account for some of the recorded sightings of water shrews in places well away from water.

Meeting to mate

Water shrews may be solitary animals, but they must meet once a year to mate. Breeding begins in April, and gestation lasts from two to three weeks. The average litter comprises six young, but sometimes ten or more babies are born. The female has five pairs of teats from which her young can suckle, two more pairs than the common shrew. Even so, large litters are unlikely to survive long in the wild.

For much of the year, water shrews look sleek and pied in appearance. During the spring moult, however, the fur can turn brown all over, with little contrast between the upper and lower parts.

On land, the water shrew eats mainly earthworms, beetles, small spiders and insect larvae. It hunts along stream banks using special runways worn through the waterside vegetation.

Many youngsters die in the first few months of independence; if they reach their first winter, they will probably survive long enough to breed.

Most water shrews die from exhaustion. The strong-smelling skin glands that all shrews possess make them unattractive prey to mammalian predators. As a result, water shrews are usually left alone and rarely eaten even when captured. Birds have a poorly developed sense of taste and are less bothered by foul odours, but nevertheless water shrews are not often eaten by owls or kestrels.

The babies weigh just about one gram (a tiny fraction of an ounce) at birth and are blind, pink and helpless. By the fourth day, they begin to darken in colour, and by about the tenth day fur has started to grow. The family leaves the nest after about three weeks, often travelling in single file, the mother leading the way and each youngster holding on to the rump of the one in front.

The young stay close to their mother until they disperse when they are about six weeks old. Their mother may then have another litter that summer; sometimes there may even be time for a

third before the season ends. This is unusual, however. Breeding is such a demanding activity that many adult females die at this time. Litters born late in the summer are generally smaller than those produced earlier in the year.

Brief lives

Some females may have their first litter in the same year as they themselves were born but most do not breed until the following year, when they are nearly one year old. Water shrews may survive into a second winter, living for 18 or 19 months, although this is unusual. Nevertheless, water shrews live longer than common shrews, which have a maximum life span of around 14 months.

In winter, most of the water shrew population consists of growing juveniles.

Like other shrews, the water shrew must spend most of its short life searching for food or it will die of starvation. Its sensory whiskers and well-developed sense of smell are both used to detect prey.

Dazzling kingfisher

Despite its fantastic iridescent plumage, the kingfisher can often be elusive. Knowing exactly where and when to look on the river bank will increase the chance of sighting this jewel-like bird.

blur of brilliant blue and orange is usually what you glimpse of a kingfisher as it flashes past, flying low over the water. You may hear its loud, sharp, high-pitched whistle nearby, which is often uttered in alarm as it heads for cover in a tree on the bank, but unless you are lucky you probably will not see the bird clearly.

A good close-up view of a kingfisher is definitely worth waiting for. It has arguably the brightest plumage of any British bird, with incredible blues and greens on its wings, back and head that change in intensity as the bird moves in the sunlight. The paler blue patch extending down the back and into the base of the tail is the feature most likely to catch your eye when a kingfisher is flying.

Brilliant camouflage

Seen close up, the kingfisher is a brilliantly coloured bird – it could almost be called gaudy – but in its natural habitat, its vibrant plumage makes it surprisingly hard to see. From the front, or below, the rusty underparts disguise the bird well against a sandy bank, mud, or twigs and branches. From above, the blue-green plumage blends with the ever-changing ripples and reflections from the surface of the water.

The kingfisher's behaviour also helps to conceal it. When sitting on a perch, it keeps very still, save for the occasional nod of its head or bob of its tail. Then when it flies, it takes off suddenly, usually flying direct and low, and quickly finding cover again, vanishing into a tangle of trees or bushes.

As it bursts from the sunlit water, the kingfisher's vivid colours blend with sparkling rainbows in the splashes. Its bright plumage also warns off predators.

Although absent from much of Scotland, the kingfisher is widespread in most of Britain and Ireland. You most commonly encounter kingfishers in their favoured habitats around lowland rivers, streams and lakes, where they are seen throughout the year. In hard winters, kingfishers abandon their usual haunts for lower, warmer ground, such as that bordering an estuary.

Records show that kingfisher numbers were badly hit during hard winters, particularly those of 1961–2, 1962–3, 1978–9 and 1981–2. At the other extreme, hot, dry conditions also affect kingfisher

KINGFISHER FACT FILE

*The kingfisher is a small, compact bird, with a disproportionately large
bill. Its plumage is bright and its flight normally rapid and straight,
usually across open water to vegetation on the banks, where it may perch
on a stump or twig, watching the water for potential prey.*

● NAMES
Common name: kingfisher
Latin name: *Alcedo atthis*

● HABITAT
Clear, unpolluted, slow-moving or still
water with suitable banks for nesting;
also along estuaries and sheltered
coasts in winter

● DISTRIBUTION
Found over much of British Isles
except northern Scotland, though most
numerous in central and southern
England and central and eastern Ireland

● STATUS
British population estimated at 4500
pairs, with further 1800 pairs in Ireland

● SIZE
Length 16–17cm (6¼–6½in),
of which about 4cm (1½in) is bill;
wingspan 24–26cm (9½–10½in);
weight 35–40g (1¼–1½oz)

● KEY FEATURES
Brilliant blue and green upper plumage,
rusty orange beneath, pattern of orange,
white and blue on head; tiny, bright
orange-red feet; long beak is all-black in
males, has red underside in females

● VOICE
Loud, shrill *chee*, sometimes repeated;
especially vocal in spring and autumn,
when it uses an aggressive, piping
shrit-it-it to warn interlopers off breeding
or overwintering territory

● FOOD
Almost exclusively small fish, but also
some aquatic insects and occasionally
molluscs, crustaceans and amphibians;
hunts from perches over water or by
hovering above water's surface

● BREEDING
Eggs laid April–July; incubation about 20
days; not unusual for a pair to have 2 or
even 3 broods in a year

● NEST
5 to 7 roundish white eggs laid in a
depression at end of a 1m (3ft 3in) long
nesting tunnel, usually dug into a sandy
or muddy river bank above water

● YOUNG
Begin to acquire feathers after 10
days and can fly 23–27 days
after hatching

*The female
kingfisher has
a red base to
the lower part
of her beak.*

*An adult kingfisher has
orange-red feet, but the
feet of a juvenile are
much duller.*

In the cramped nesting chamber, young
kingfishers *churr* excitedly as a parent returns
with a fish. The chicks take it in turns to come
to the front of the queue to receive food.

Distribution map key

Present
all year round

Not present

PROTECTED!

Once persecuted
by fishermen,
kingfishers declined
through much of
their range. Now
the species enjoys full
legal protection and
must not be harmed
in any way.

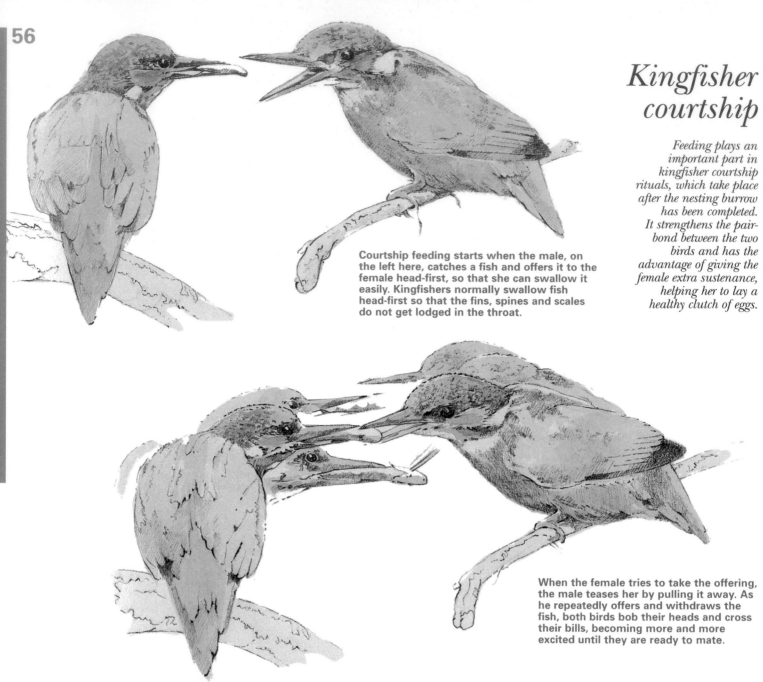

Kingfisher courtship

Feeding plays an important part in kingfisher courtship rituals, which take place after the nesting burrow has been completed. It strengthens the pair-bond between the two birds and has the advantage of giving the female extra sustenance, helping her to lay a healthy clutch of eggs.

Courtship feeding starts when the male, on the left here, catches a fish and offers it to the female head-first, so that she can swallow it easily. Kingfishers normally swallow fish head-first so that the fins, spines and scales do not get lodged in the throat.

When the female tries to take the offering, the male teases her by pulling it away. As he repeatedly offers and withdraws the fish, both birds bob their heads and cross their bills, becoming more and more excited until they are ready to mate.

numbers. Low water levels in streams and rivers concentrate the effects of pollution, and the flow becomes very irregular or even dries up altogether.

Breeding rates
Numbers recover quickly, thanks to a high breeding rate – six or seven chicks in a brood are not unusual. Occasionally, in a good year, a pair of kingfishers may raise three or even four families. Current estimates put the British population of kingfishers at around 4500 pairs, and that of Ireland at about 1800 pairs. The highest densities are in central and southern England and central and eastern Ireland.

The breeding season begins early in the year. As early as January or February, pairs start displaying to each other by bobbing heads and chasing one another around. Sometimes the male presents the female with a fish, a gesture known as courtship feeding, which helps to bond the pair.

As the warmer weather returns in spring, a pair of kingfishers starts to look

for a suitable steep bank in which to excavate a nest tunnel. Adult kingfishers are highly territorial, and each pair defends its nesting area energetically. Kingfishers can be very aggressive towards other kingfishers invading their space.

The nesting site is typically a low, almost vertical mud or sand bank, ideally with water beneath. This provides a natural moat to deter predators such as stoats, weasels and rats. If the water level drops or the stream dries up, however, the nest becomes more accessible, and the brood is more likely to be lost.

Excavating a nest
To start the tunnel off, the birds launch themselves at the bank, using their beaks as flying picks to loosen the earth. Both sexes excavate the tunnel, digging out the soil with their beaks and pushing the loose sand away with their short legs and small feet. The tunnel is normally about 1m (3ft) long, running at a slight upwards tilt into the bank. The birds open out a

nest chamber at the far end of the burrow. There, the female kingfisher lays between five and seven pinkish white eggs, usually some time between April and July.

The newly hatched chicks are blind and naked at first. In the early days, while the hatchlings are tiny, both parents select insects and the smallest fish to feed them. By the time the nestlings are ten days old, their eyes are open and they are covered in a spiky coat of blue and orange feathers still tightly wrapped in sheaths. Now the hungry chicks can cope with larger prey; they feed voraciously and keep calling for more with a constant, purring note.

The tunnel soon becomes soiled with the young birds' droppings, and also with the regurgitated bones and scales of the many fish brought in by the parents. With as many as seven young in the nest, each consuming 12 to 18 fish a day, the parents must work hard. They may have to catch up to 100 fish a day, not including the ones that they need to feed themselves.

A kingfisher approaches its nesting burrow with a fish in its beak. The nest quickly becomes fouled with regurgitated fish bones and scales, as well as the chicks' droppings. When they are strong enough, the chicks shuffle backwards to the edge of the nest chamber and squirt their excreta down the tunnel towards the light. The slight slope from the chamber to the entrance helps the foul-smelling liquid to drain away. The waste eventually trickles out of the entrance hole and leaves conspicuous white streaks running down the riverbank.

When both birds are ready to mate, the male finally allows the female to take the fish he is proffering. The female then moves to sit beside the male.

The female turns her back on the male and adopts a submissive posture. The male kingfisher then mounts his partner, holding on to her head with his beak and flapping his wings to help keep his balance until mating is over.

Between 23 and 27 days after hatching, the young birds fledge and emerge from the dark, smelly nesting tunnel into the daylight for the first time and fly to a nearby perch. The parents continue to feed their brood near the nest until the youngsters are able to fish for themselves. Then the adults start to drive the young away with a combination of threat gestures and hot pursuits. Evicted from their parents' territory, the young birds have to find new stretches of water to make their own. They may have to travel many miles to find a suitable site that is not already occupied by another pair of kingfishers.

Favourite foods

Kingfishers eat mainly small fish, including the young of larger fish species, but they also take aquatic insect larvae and insects from land. Although a kingfisher may take

When hunting, a kingfisher sits upright on a favoured perch about 1m (3ft) above the surface, head tilted down as it scans the water for potential prey. On spying a fish, the bird tenses and tilts its body. In so doing, it is able to gauge the angle and direction of its imminent dive.

The kingfisher then flies strongly into the water, at an angle of about 45°. If the fish has moved far, the dive may be preceded by a brief hover a little way out from the perch, as the kingfisher reassesses the situation. As the bird enters the water, it uses its tail to fine-tune its direction.

the occasional young trout from a fish-farm, or goldfish from a garden pond, the species poses little commercial threat or nuisance to anglers. The loss of a few fish seems a small price to pay for the privilege of regular sightings of such a beautiful bird.

The kingfishers' favoured method of feeding is to sit on a branch or twig overhanging the water, or occasionally on a boulder, and wait until a suitably sized fish swims underneath. If no convenient perch is available, the bird may fly above the water, hovering briefly to get a fix on its target before diving from midair.

Kingfishers spend a lot of time preening and cleaning their plumage, especially after getting their feathers wet by diving for food. The feathers also get dirty when the birds are digging their nesting tunnel. A kingfisher washes itself by making repeated short dives into the water,

interspersed with bouts of preening to tidy the feathers and re-oil the plumage in order to keep it waterproof. At the end of a preening session, the bird stretches its wings and opens its beak wide, as if it is yawning, then flies off to go fishing again.

Threats to kingfishers

Kingfishers used to be persecuted by fishermen, and were also shot or trapped for their feathers, which were prized by the fashion industry and by anglers, who used them in tying artificial flies. However, since 1954, kingfishers have been protected by law in the UK.

A far greater threat now comes from loss of habitat and interference with the kingfisher's environment. So-called river improvement schemes, which involve straightening streams and rivers and the reinforcing of river banks, reduce natural tree cover and the availability of suitable

banks for nest sites. This type of disruption can also scare away the kingfisher's prey.

Pollution is another significant threat, since it reduces the number and variety of fish in a stream or river. Many stretches of water have lost their kingfisher populations through an increase in industrial and domestic waste and acid rain, or from agricultural fertilizers entering the water. Kingfishers may also be directly poisoned by pesticides. On the bright side, these birds are frequently quick to re-establish themselves on rivers and streams that have been cleaned up and where strict pollution controls have been enforced.

Perhaps the single most important check on the number of kingfishers is an entirely natural one – harsh weather in winter. When the water freezes over kingfishers cannot fish, and many starve to death during prolonged icy spells.

Where can I see kingfishers?

● You can find kingfishers in most of Britain and Ireland, around lowland rivers, streams and lakes. They are less common in northern parts.

● The birds like water bordered by lots of vegetation, so look around more sheltered banks. If the weather is very cold, you may see kingfishers fishing around estuaries or near the coast.

● Go out early in the morning to watch for kingfishers, preferably before there are many people around – particularly people walking their dogs – as kingfishers are wary and sensitive to noise.

● Scanning likely riverside perches with binoculars is a good way to spy on a kingfisher without disturbing it. Then, keeping it in view, you can slowly move forward into a better position without scaring the bird into flying off into cover.

● If you hear a whistle, or see a kingfisher streak away, it is often worth settling down nearby and waiting patiently. After a while, the kingfisher usually returns to the same place, or to a spot nearby, to continue fishing.

With eyes closed, the kingfisher seizes its prey in its powerful bill. It bobs straight back to the surface and flies off, the fish still wriggling, to a nearby perch. Here, the kingfisher bashes the fish against the perch until it is dead, before either swallowing it head-first or taking it back to the nest to feed hungry chicks.

By no means is every dive successful, and a kingfisher often emerges from the water with an empty beak. An experienced adult bird can usually expect to catch a fish every second or third dive. When a young kingfisher starts diving, however, it misses its target far more frequently. Judging the precise speed and angle of attack, and allowing for the distorting effect of the air–water interface, are skills that must be honed with practice.

Recognising surface-feeding ducks

The brightly coloured plumage of the male ducks means they are easy to identify as they dabble in ponds, streams and rivers, but the subtler colours of the females make them trickier to distinguish.

Few birds are more relaxing to watch than ducks. Their special appeal stems in part from their pleasing shape and attractive mix of colours.

The surface-feeding or dabbling ducks, a group of species belonging to the genus *Anas*, are so called because they tend to feed at the water's surface, upending in shallow water to reach the bottom without submerging. They dive underwater only very occasionally, mostly to escape predators.

Most people will be familiar with at least some members of this group, which includes the mallard and the teal. One of Britain's largest duck species, the shelduck, is also included here. Although belonging to a different group, it is a surface feeder.

Apart from the garganey – a scarce passage migrant in spring and autumn, which rarely breeds in the UK – most surface feeders are relatively widespread and seasonally common. This allows many opportunities to observe these engaging creatures in and around the ponds and rivers, lakes, wetlands and nature reserves of Britain. Although generally gregarious during winter, many ducks tend to be more solitary during the breeding season.

In general, female surface-feeding ducks are the most difficult to distinguish from each other, largely because, whatever the species, their plumage is a similar brownish hue. Their muted colouring serves a specific purpose during the breeding season: blending into the background helps the mother bird to protect herself and her precious nest of eggs. The exception to this rule is the shelduck, where both sexes are boldly marked and rather similar in colouring throughout the year.

Dramatic moult

Male surface-feeding ducks generally have two plumages. From late autumn to early summer they are resplendent in full breeding plumage, displaying many colours and patterns in their attempts to attract a mate.

From late summer to early autumn, however, the males moult and acquire a plumage similar to the females of their species, known as an 'eclipse'. Also, for a short period every one of them is flightless until their new wing feathers grow.

At this time of year, moulted feathers lying on the bank can provide clues as to the identity of any ducks in the vicinity.

Male surface-feeding ducks play no part in making the nest or incubating the eggs. The nest is a simple affair, typically a well-concealed depression in the ground lined with vegetation and soft down feathers from the female's breast. The exception among the ducks described here is the shelduck, which nests in a ready-made burrow or hole, lined with down.

Males often stand guard in the vicinity of the eggs after breeding, which can make them easy to observe. Remember not to get too close, however, since you might frighten one or both parents away, leaving the eggs even more vulnerable.

The female mallard has sole responsibility for the rearing of ducklings. Her brood follows her wherever she goes and the ducklings stay with her until they fledge, up to 60 days after hatching.

EASY GUIDE TO SURFACE-FEEDING DUCKS

Female
Mallard
Male

Male
Female
Gadwall

Male
Female
Garganey

Male
Female
Pintail

Male
Female
Wigeon

Male
Female
Shoveler

Female   Male
Teal

Male
Shelduck

WHAT ARE SURFACE-FEEDING DUCKS?

● Surface-feeding ducks have broad, flattened bills that are suited to sifting through shallow waters and surface layers of estuary and marshland mud, collecting minute animals as well as plant material.

● Throughout Britain, seven of the eight regular species of surface-feeding ducks (above) are relatively wide-spread; they all belong to the family Anatidae and are otherwise known as wildfowl. All except for the shelduck are dabbling ducks.

● Unlike marine ducks, surface-feeding ducks walk on land with comparative ease – although all have a characteristic waddling gait.

◄ Showing off the pointed tail after which it is named, this drake pintail has upended to search for food.

▲ A young shelduck sifts through silt in the shallows for tiny water snails and other invertebrates.

HOW TO IDENTIFY SURFACE-FEEDING DUCKS

● The males (also known as drakes) of all surface-feeding duck species are usually easy to identify, since all have conspicuous and often colourful plumage patterns for most of the year.

● Females are more of a challenge to identify, although fortunately they invariably consort with males of their own kind, even outside the breeding season.

● All the dabbling ducks (genus *Anas*) form flocks outside the breeding season. Shelducks are most inclined to congregate during the late summer

The sexes of most surface-feeding ducks have strikingly different plumages. Here, a male mallard (left) stands next to his rather sombre plumaged mate.

when they gather in safe areas to moult.

● Another useful aid to identification is the flight pattern on the upperwings of both sexes: each species has unique markings on the inner wing and, in some, iridescent secondary flight feathers form a colourful panel called the wing patch or speculum. This patch is often framed by white lines on both the leading and trailing edges of the wing.

WILDLIFE WATCH

When and where can I find surface-feeding ducks?

Since many surface-feeding ducks found in Britain breed farther north in Europe, and those that remain are extremely secretive when nesting, summer is not always the easiest time to observe them. Some of the more common species, however, can be seen throughout the spring and summer months.

● Mallards can be found in almost any relatively undisturbed freshwater habitat throughout the year. They can also be found on the coast during winter.

● Gadwall are typically found in flooded gravel pits and reservoirs although they also occur on natural lakes. They are scarce but widely scattered, breeding mostly in East Anglia.

● Pintails are found on flooded wetlands and estuaries. They rarely breed in Britain, except in Scotland, and the breeding population does not often reach 50 pairs. Look for them in flocks between September and April.

● Garganey are best spotted during their spring and autumn migration, although they

occasionally breed here. Look for them on flooded wetlands from March to May and in August and September.

● Shovelers favour shallow lakes and flooded meadows and are commonest between October and March.

● Teal are found in similar habitats to wigeon, but are more widespread as breeders.

● Wigeon occur in large flocks on estuaries and flooded wetlands between late August and early April.

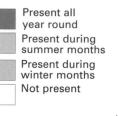

Distribution map key

■	Present all year round
■	Present during summer months
■	Present during winter months
□	Not present

MALLARD *Anas platyrhynchos*

This is Britain's best-known duck. The breeding male has an iridescent green head, dark chestnut breast and grey-brown body. The female has mottled brown plumage, as does the eclipse male (but with a yellow bill). In flight, all birds show a bright purple-blue wing patch with a white border.

The beautifully marked head of the male mallard is bordered by a white neck ring.

Female

Dark orange bill

Yellow bill

Black and white on stern

Orange legs

Male

● SIZE
Length 50–62cm (20–24½in), wingspan 81–95cm (32–37½in)

● NEST
In a depression among vegetation

● BREEDING
Lays 9–13 eggs, mainly April–May; incubation takes about 27 days

● FOOD
Omnivorous diet, includes seeds, shoots and small aquatic animals

● HABITAT
All types of freshwater habitats during the breeding season; occurs near coasts in winter

● VOICE
Female in particular utters the familiar quack; male quietly whistles, grunts and makes nasal calls

● STATUS
Widespread and common in most parts of Britain and throughout the year

GADWALL *Anas strepera*

A compact duck with subdued markings that forms flocks on open water when not breeding. The male is generally grey-brown except for a dark bill. Females are similar to the female mallard, but an orange band runs along the side of the bill. The eclipse male is similar to the female but darker. In flight, a white patch, bordered with black, can be seen on the rear of the inner wing.

At close range, the delicate markings on the body of this male gadwall can be seen to good effect; note the black stern.

Orange stripe on bill

Female

Prominent dark stern

Body mainly grey with fine markings

Male

● SIZE
Length 46–56cm (18–22in), wingspan78–90cm (30¾–35½in)

● NEST
On ground, among vegetation

● BREEDING
Lays 8–12 eggs, mainly May–June; incubation takes about 25 days

● FOOD
Seeds, shoots and insects

● HABITAT
Freshwater wetlands during breeding season; lakes and flooded gravel pits in winter

● VOICE
Male has a nasal croak; female has a soft quack

● STATUS
Scarce breeding species but widespread and more common throughout winter

PINTAIL *Anas acuta*

The distinctive, long-bodied pintail forms loose flocks in winter on estuaries and wetlands. The male has a chocolate-brown head, grey bill, white front and neck stripe with a mainly grey body and dark legs. Its longer tail feathers are often held erect. The female is a mottled buff-brown, with a dark grey bill and legs. The eclipse male is similar to the female. In flight, the male has a dull bronze-green wing patch, while the female's is brownish.

Grey bill

Striking white stripe extends up side of neck

Male

Female

At all times pintails look elongated and slim.

● **SIZE**
Length 51–62cm (20¼–24½in), wingspan 79-87cm (31–34¼in)

● **NEST**
Placed in fairly open site among wetland vegetation

● **BREEDING**
Lays 7–9 eggs, mainly April–May; incubation takes about 23 days

● **FOOD**
Seeds, plant shoots and insects

● **HABITAT**
Breeds on undisturbed wetlands; winters on lakes and estuaries

● **VOICE**
Male utters soft, low whistling calls; female utters short, hoarse low quacks

● **STATUS**
Rare breeding species; fairly common winter visitor

GARGANEY *Anas querquedula*

Only a little larger than a teal, the adult male has a reddish brown head, neck and breast, and a white eyestripe, the rest of its body is greyish brown. The female looks like the teal, but with distinctive face markings. In flight, both sexes show a blue-grey upper forewing, but it is brighter in the males.

Pale spot at base of bill, dark eyestripe and cheeks

Female

Male

Pinkish brown breast

Long shoulder feathers form pale stripes on back

The male garganey is easy to recognise, thanks to its conspicuous white 'eyebrow' or supercilium.

● **SIZE**
Length 37–41cm (14½–16¼in), wingspan 60–65cm (24–25½in)

● **NEST**
On ground, in waterside vegetation

● **BREEDING**
Lays 8–11 eggs, mainly April–May; incubation takes about 22 days

● **FOOD**
Aquatic plants and insects

● **HABITAT**
Flood meadows and wetlands

● **VOICE**
Male utters dry rattling call, female a short, sharp quack

● **STATUS**
Rare breeding species; scarce but regular passage migrant in spring and autumn

SHOVELER *Anas clypeata*

The shoveler has a huge, flattened bill. The adult male has a dark green head and neck, white breast and rear flanks, a bright chestnut belly and black stern. Its bill is black and its legs orange. The female is a mottled reddish brown, her bill dark with orange sides, her legs a dull orange. The eclipse male is similar to the female. In flight, both sexes show a pale blue shoulder patch separated from a green wing patch by a white band; the female's is duller in colour.

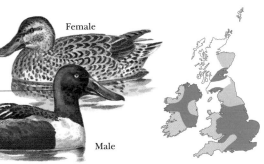

Long, broad bill is distinctive in both sexes

Female

Contrasting plumage colours

Male

Even though the shoveler swims low in the water, its chestnut flanks framed by white, can aid identification.

● **SIZE**
Length 44–52cm (17½–20½in), wingspan 73–82cm (28¾–32¼in)

● **NEST**
In depression among wetland vegetation

● **BREEDING**
Lays 8–12 eggs, mainly April–May; incubation about 22 days

● **FOOD**
Small aquatic invertebrates and plant shoots

● **HABITAT**
Shallow lakes, flooded meadows and estuaries

● **VOICE**
Male utters soft 'took-took'; female utters hoarse, wheezy calls and soft quacks

● **STATUS**
Scarce breeding species but common winter visitor in favoured areas

TEAL   *Anas crecca*

Britain's smallest duck forms large, fast-flying flocks outside
the breeding season. The adult male has a chestnut head and
neck, and a green patch with a yellow border around the eye.
Its body is grey with fine, intricate markings, its stern yellow
with a black border. The bill and legs are dark grey. The
female is mottled grey-brown, with a dark grey bill. In flight,
both sexes show a green wing patch.

Plumage mottled grey-brown

Female

Black and yellow colours on stern

Male

● **SIZE**
Length 34–38cm (13½–15in),
wingspan 53–59cm (20¾–23¼in)

● **NEST**
On ground, in deep cover

● **BREEDING**
Lays 8–11 eggs, mainly May;
incubation takes about 22 days

● **FOOD**
Seeds, plant shoots and
small invertebrates

**What it lacks in size, the
male teal makes up for
with beautiful plumage.**

● **HABITAT**
Freshwater
wetlands
in breeding
season; in winter, also
on estuaries and
flooded grassland

● **VOICE**
Male utters a
high-pitched,
piping '*kriik*';
female utters
soft quacks

● **STATUS**
A fairly common breeding species;
widespread and numerous in winter

SHELDUCK   *Tadorna tadorna*

One of Britain's largest species, both sexes have a distinctive
dark iridescent green head, neck and bands down the back,
a chestnut breast band and are white elsewhere. The legs are
reddish pink, the bill red (the male shows a red knob at the
base of the bill, whereas the female usually has some white).
Juveniles have much white about the head and underparts.
In flight, all birds look strikingly black and white.

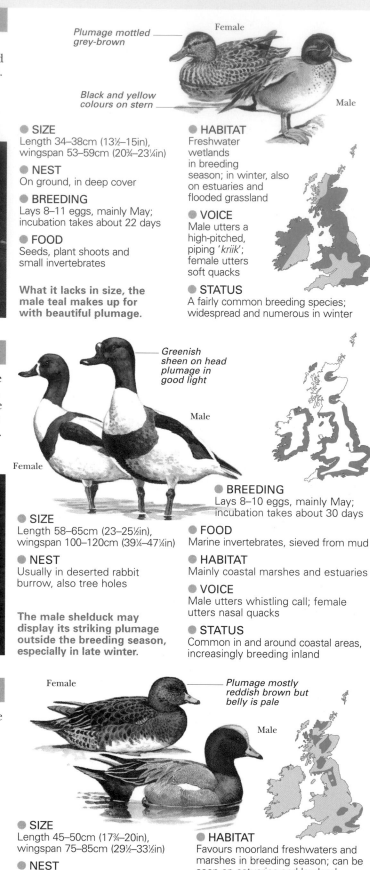

Greenish sheen on head plumage in good light

Male

Female

● **SIZE**
Length 58–65cm (23–25½in),
wingspan 100–120cm (39¼–47¼in)

● **NEST**
Usually in deserted rabbit
burrow, also tree holes

**The male shelduck may
display its striking plumage
outside the breeding season,
especially in late winter.**

● **BREEDING**
Lays 8–10 eggs, mainly May;
incubation takes about 30 days

● **FOOD**
Marine invertebrates, sieved from mud

● **HABITAT**
Mainly coastal marshes and estuaries

● **VOICE**
Male utters whistling call; female
utters nasal quacks

● **STATUS**
Common in and around coastal areas,
increasingly breeding inland

WIGEON   *Anas penelope*

A familiar winter visitor to coasts and wetlands, the adult male
wigeon has an orange-chestnut head with a pale yellow blaze
on its forehead. Its breast is pinkish, otherwise the body is
grey and finely marked with a black-and-white pattern on the
stern. The female has grey-brown, marbled plumage with a
white belly and dark eyepatch. The eclipse male is similar to
the female, but with warmer brown plumage. In flight, the
male shows a white shoulder patch and a green wing patch.
The female has a pale brown shoulder patch.

Female

Plumage mostly reddish brown but belly is pale

Male

**All wigeon
have dark-
tipped
grey bills.
They feed
both in
shallow
waters and
on land.**

● **SIZE**
Length 45–50cm (17¾–20in),
wingspan 75–85cm (29½–33½in)

● **NEST**
On ground, in cover of vegetation

● **BREEDING**
Lays 6–12 eggs, mainly June;
incubation takes about 25 days

● **FOOD**
Mainly plant material; grains,
plant shoots; eelgrass favoured
on estuaries

● **HABITAT**
Favours moorland freshwaters and
marshes in breeding season; can be
seen on estuaries and lowland
wetlands in winter

● **VOICE**
Male utters '*whee-ooo*' call; female
utters grating purr

● **STATUS**
Scarce breeding species but
widespread winter visitor

The grass snake

The shy grass snake – the largest snake in Britain – is usually found near or in water. Frogs are its main food, and it will swim through plants at the water's edge of ponds and streams to find them.

Out of almost 3000 species of snake worldwide, just three are native to Britain – the grass snake, the smooth snake and the adder. All of these are widely distributed across Europe – the grass snake is found as far east as western Asia. Contrary to popular perception, 80 per cent of all snake species are harmless to humans. Although grass snakes do produce a toxic secretion from a special gland in the upper jaw, they hardly ever bite and are not considered venomous.

Like other reptiles, snakes are cold-blooded or, to use the scientific term, ectothermic. This means that, unlike mammals and birds, they are unable to maintain a high body temperature by generating heat internally from the metabolism of food. To raise their temperature before they can become active, grass snakes must bask in the sun; in winter they need to hibernate to avoid being frozen.

Southern bias

The grass snake is fairly hardy and capable of enduring the cool climates of Britain and northern Europe. For reasons not well understood, it is not normally found in Scotland. Those that have been recorded north of the border are pets that have been released or have escaped.

While the grass snake may swallow tadpoles as it swims along, it takes full-grown frogs ashore to eat them.

Grass snakes were once commonly known as 'ringed snakes'. This old-fashioned name is far more descriptive of their appearance than the modern alternative, as most individuals possess a distinctive yellow collar around the neck. While grass snakes are certainly found in grassy areas, they are encountered chiefly in wet surroundings, on moors, heaths and downland, and in quarries, hedgerows and woods. The snake's scientific name, *Natrix*, is derived from the Latin *nato*, meaning 'I swim', and reflects its predominantly aquatic habits.

Like most snakes, grass snakes feed on a wide selection of prey, ranging from earthworms to bird's eggs and small mammals. They eat dead animals too, as

The grass snake's forked tongue is constantly darting in and out of its mouth. This may seem intimidating, but the snake is simply sampling the air to find out what is going on around it.

long as the corpses have not started to decompose. Perhaps the most bizarre prey so far recorded has been honey bees.

Given their aquatic tendencies, it is hardly surprising that grass snakes feed mainly on amphibians and small fish. A grass snake is known to have eaten nine

DID YOU KNOW?

Although grass snakes are not usually found close to the sea, the occasional individual has been found swimming offshore. One was even caught about 23km (14 miles) from the nearest land.

GRASS SNAKE FACT FILE

Britain's longest and most aquatic snake, the grass snake is commonly found in lowland areas and is rare in the north. It often lives near water in damp grass and ditches, beside ponds and slow-moving streams, where it hunts mainly for frogs and toads.

● NAMES
Common names: grass snake, ringed snake, common snake, green snake, hedge snake, water snake
Scientific name: *Natrix natrix*

● HABITAT
Wetlands, including damp meadows, marshes or close to ponds, rivers, streams, ditches and canals; favours sunny areas near thick grass or the cover of bushes

● DISTRIBUTION
Mainly lowlands, in southern and central England and Wales including Anglesey, though rare in mid-Wales; rare or absent from much of northern England, virtually absent from Scotland; absent from Ireland and also the Isle of Man; the only snake in Jersey, Channel Islands

● STATUS
Around 320,000 in Britain

● SIZE
Female length up to 120cm (3ft 9in) or more; male up to 80cm (2ft 7½in) or slightly more

● KEY FEATURES
Olive green to brown or grey above, with row of regular, vertical, black bars along flanks, 2 rows of smaller black spots on back; 2 black, crescent-shaped marks behind head, in front of which is a yellow, white or pink collar; belly is chequered black or grey on a white background; throat white or yellow; males and females similar in appearance

● HABITS
Cold blooded; hibernates October–early March or early April in secure crevices in walls, among boulders or tree roots; most active in warmer weather; normally found close to water; hunts on land and in water, may climb trees

● VOICE
Loud hiss when threatened

● FOOD
Frogs, toads, newts, fish and sometimes lizards, young birds, mice, voles, shrews; young eat tadpoles, worms and slugs

● BREEDING
Male is sexually mature at around 3 years, female at 4–5 years; mating occurs April–early June; 40 or more eggs usually laid June–July, occasionally in August, rarely even later; young hatch late August–early September, occasionally in October

● NEST
Eggs laid in warm, humid chamber in compost or manure heap, haystack, tree hole or abandoned mammal burrow

● YOUNG
Born 2 months after eggs are laid, measure 14–21cm (5½–8¼in) in length; young look like miniature adults, although slightly darker with less well-defined markings

● SIGNS
Sloughed skins; burrows in compost heaps; remains of eggshells from previous season

Two months after the eggs are laid, young grass snakes emerge from the leathery shells. Warmed by the late summer sunshine, they set off hunting almost straightaway.

Distribution map key

■	Present
□	Not present

The upperside is olive brown, while the belly is chequered black or grey on white.

There is a row of regular, vertical black bars along each flank, and two rows of alternate spots on the back.

A pair of crescent-shaped yellow patches in front of a pair of crescent-shaped black patches mark the nape.

The pupils of the eyes are rounded, unlike those of the adder, which are slit-shaped.

PROTECTED!

Grass snakes are protected under Schedule 5 of the Wildlife and Countryside Act 1981, which outlaws their deliberate killing, injury or sale.

In a confrontation with a grass snake, a frog is likely to come off worse. Grass snakes can eat as many as four or five adult frogs in quick succession, or up to 20 small ones. Two grass snakes managed to devour 108 frogs in four months.

gudgeon in a matter of hours. Fish are swallowed head-first so that the bones of the fins do not stick in the snake's throat.

Frogs form the bulk of most adult grass snakes' diet, while juveniles often prey on tadpoles. The snake can swallow frogs whole because it has a very wide gape: both sides of the upper and lower jaws can be moved independently, or even dislocated if necessary, to accommodate large prey.

In turn, grass snakes themselves are preyed upon by a number of predatory birds and mammals, such as hedgehogs and badgers. They appear to be immune to the bite of the adder, however, and rarely succumb to them.

Although they are naturally inoffensive and rarely bite, grass snakes may give the impression of being ferocious by inflating their bodies, hissing loudly and striking out with their mouths closed. Such extreme behaviour usually occurs only

when the snake is cornered, as it would normally prefer to slip away into the vegetation or disappear underwater, sometimes remaining submerged for as long as an hour.

Alternatively, the grass snake may play dead, turning over on its back, letting its body go limp, with its long tongue drooping from gaping jaws. This trick might buy a little escape time from a bemused predator. If turned the right way up again, the grass snake immediately resumes its 'dead' position.

A more usual means of defence is to struggle violently when caught, discharging a foul-smelling fluid and simultaneously defecating. It may also regurgitate its last meal.

The great escape

A toad is a good catch for the grass snake, even though the warty amphibian produces noxious skin secretions. One toad can satisfy a snake's hunger for a week to 10 days. The toad resorts to some evasive protection ploys before it simply turns and runs.

When confronted with a grass snake, a toad remains motionless, hoping that the sinuous predator will simply slither past.

If the snake persists, the toad inflates its body with air and raises itself off the ground in order to appear as large and unswallowable as possible.

If all else fails, the toad turns and hops or swims away. The grass snake is unlikely to pursue it for long, as it prefers to hunt by stealth and to ambush its prey.

FOLKLORE

According to folklore, grass snakes suckle milk from cow's udders, a habit also attributed to slow-worms. However, research has shown that grass snakes have no interest in drinking milk. It is most likely that this belief arose because snakes were seen seeking shelter and warmth beside sleeping cows.

Like all snakes, grass snakes have been needlessly persecuted over the years, usually in the unfounded belief that they have a poisonous sting on their tongue. Grass snakes found in houses and gardens are often killed through fear and ignorance. Not only is this pointless but it is against the law. The grass snake needs help and protection if it is to continue to be part of the British countryside.

Joys of spring

From early March, when grass snakes begin to emerge from hibernation, groups that have shared the same den over the winter can occasionally be discovered basking together. Males and females are very similar, although females are longer.

Mating occurs from April to early June and is quite a low-key affair. Unlike adders, male grass snakes do not indulge in ritualised trials of strength. Indeed, they seem almost totally indifferent to one another. The male follows the female, rubbing his chin on her back and flicking his tongue, although sometimes even these basic preliminaries are dispensed with. The two snakes mate with the ends of their bodies and tails entwined.

Sexual behaviour seems to be stimulated by warm weather and usually occurs when temperatures reach 18–21°C (64–70°F). A female grass snake may mate three times during the mating season, then lay her eggs about two months later. The grass snake is unique among British snakes in that it lays eggs rather than producing live young.

Despite an affinity with water, when it comes to breeding the grass snake often seeks out farmyards or gardens. Eggs are laid beneath tree roots or in disused burrows, but what the female snake is really looking for is a site where heat is generated by rotting vegetation. Compost and manure heaps are ideal, or under hayricks and piles of sawdust. Females may travel over half a mile from their usual haunts to find a suitable incubator. They have even been found nesting in wall cavities and near a baker's oven.

▲ In June or July, a fully grown female grass snake lays up to 40 matt white eggs, although as many as 53 have been recorded in a single clutch. It may take her up to 12 hours to lay the whole clutch.

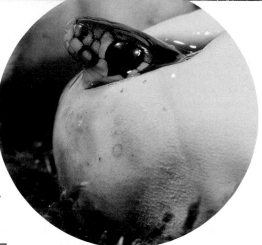

▶ Most young grass snakes hatch in late August or early September. The miniature grass snake slashes its way out of the egg by using its egg-tooth to cut slits in the leathery shell.

▼ Having few other means of self-defence, a grass snake often plays dead when threatened by a predator. It looks dramatic, flopped on its back, with its mouth open, tongue lolling and eyes staring.

▲ Being cold-blooded, a grass snake has to raise its body temperature by basking in the sun. Rocky places are good for sunbathing as the stone absorbs heat, so the snake's body is warmed from above and below. On hot days, it seeks shade to avoid overheating.

▼ Sloughing its skin is an energetic exercise for a snake. While it is still growing, a young grass snake sheds its skin three to 12 times a year but once sexually mature the males slough twice a year, females once.

▶ Before it is shed, the skin becomes dark and dull and the eyes look opaque as the transparent scale protecting them loosens. Immediately after sloughing, the grass snake's colouring is at its brightest.

Once a nest site has been found, the female grass snake burrows in and creates a chamber by curling up into a ball and wriggling around.

Suitable laying sites are often few and far between, so a single den may be used by several females. Up to a thousand eggs have been discovered at some sites; when so many young snakes hatch at once, it seems like a 'plague' of snakes.

Grass snake eggs are unlikely to hatch at temperatures below 20°C (68°F), and temperatures within compost heaps can reach 40°C (104°F). Hatching takes six to eight weeks. Development in the egg is dependent upon temperature, eggs laid

▶ The grass snake twists around to rub the loose scales off in one piece, and its sloughed skin is sometimes found intact. Even so, it is hard to distinguish a grass snake's skin from another species without knowing the arrangement of the head scales.

in warm nests requiring less incubation time than those laid in cooler places.

Larger females lay more eggs than smaller ones. One egg is laid about every five minutes. As they are laid, a sticky secretion glues the eggs together into a cluster. The matt white eggs have leathery shells and measure 15 x 25mm (⅝ x 1in).

WILDLIFE WATCH

Where can I find grass snakes?

● Like all our native reptiles, grass snakes are timid creatures and as such are rarely seen. The best time to look for them is early in the morning during late spring and summer. Cloudy days with sunny spells are ideal, since the snakes are obliged to take advantage of any sunshine to bask in the open.

● Garden ponds often attract grass snakes, especially if they are home to frogs and tadpoles. There is little you can do to protect the amphibians in your garden, and if a snake has a successful hunt, it will probably make return trips. But do not despair – a visiting grass snake is the ultimate seal of approval for any wildlife pond.

◀ To swallow a frog whole and alive, a grass snake opens its mouth to maximum gape and dislocates its jaws, then glides over its still struggling victim.

As the eggs develop they absorb water and increase in length to 40mm (1½in). Females occasionally remain near the eggs for a few days, but there is little evidence that they are actually guarding the nest. They may simply be exhausted by the exertions of egg laying.

All the eggs in one brood usually hatch within a few hours of each other. Young grass snakes break out of their eggs using an egg-tooth, located just below the tip of the nose, to cut through the shell. The egg-tooth drops off within 12 hours of hatching. Newly emerged grass snakes are 14–21cm (5½–8¼in) long.

Sensory perceptions

In common with other snakes, a grass snake relies on its sight and on information gathered from its surroundings with its tongue to locate prey. Vision is the main method by which the snake locates its prey, but when the snake nears its quarry, the sense of smell becomes more important in determining what the prey is and if it is edible. The grass snake habitually flicks its white-

▶ Grass snakes are surprisingly good climbers and sometimes rest among tree branches in the cool shade. Once there, they may take advantage of the opportunity to raid birds' nests for eggs and chicks.

tipped tongue, more frequently than either the adder or the smooth snake.

As with all snakes, the eyes of the grass snake have no eyelids; instead each eye is protected by a transparent scale, the brille, which is shed at the same time as the snake sheds its skin. Unlike lizards, snakes have no eardrums or external ears. They do, however, have an internal ear bone, the stapes. This is attached to the bone of the upper jaw, which is in turn connected to the lower jaw. This arrangement suggests that snakes do not hear sounds, such as a human voice, passing through the air, but detect vibrations conducted through the surface on which they are resting. These vibrations are relayed via the lower jaw to the other two bones. Sounds transmitted through the ground act as a warning system of approaching danger.

▼ A grass snake swims with sinuous grace, using side-to-side undulations of its long, muscular body to propel itself swiftly through the water. Its head is held above the water's surface.

The edible frog

Once the breeding season begins, the male edible frog is difficult to miss. From his perch alongside a pool or stream, he serenades the female with loud, staccato calls that can carry for a hundred metres and more.

The edible frog is one of the green frogs, a group also known as water frogs that includes pool and marsh frogs. By contrast, Britain's most widespread native frog, the common frog, belongs to a group popularly known as brown frogs.

Pool and marsh frogs are widespread in Europe and, where they occur together, they sometimes interbreed, giving rise to the edible frog. Unusually for a hybrid, an edible frog can breed with either parent species to produce more edible frogs.

Green frogs have been introduced to Britain at various times in small numbers and restricted locations, mostly in the south and east of England, but also in Lancashire and Yorkshire. Most introductions have taken place in Kent, where green frogs have been recorded in at least 288 sites. As a result, edible, pool and marsh frogs are well established.

Peaceful habitats

All green frogs live along watercourses such as drainage channels, neglected canals, weed-infested backwaters of larger rivers and sheltered lake margins. Quiet waterways where they can bask in the sun on the water's edge are ideal sites. Edible frogs prefer to stay near water, often sitting on branches directly above open

The male edible frog's loud mating calls are produced by his large, inflatable vocal sacs.

pools so they can drop to safety at the first sign of danger. They are generally more aquatic in their habits than common frogs, which can be found at considerable distances from water, in woodlands and damp meadows. This means the two do not compete for food or breeding sites.

Temperate winters have encouraged the common frog to start breeding in February and March, while the edible frog and its green cousins rarely spawn before May. By this time the tadpoles of common frogs are well developed.

Edible frogs usually spend the winter months underwater, hibernating at the bottom of muddy pools and ditches. When the water temperature rises to

In mixed colonies, edible frogs may hibernate alongside pool frogs, such as the one pictured on the left, or marsh frogs, and interbreed the following year.

DID YOU KNOW?

The only parts of a frog that are eaten are the hind legs, which are long and muscular. Theoretically, any European frog's legs can be eaten, but only the edible and marsh frogs' hind legs are big enough. In Europe, large numbers are collected each year and this, together with the loss of habitat in some areas, has resulted in several species' decline in range and numbers. The reverse is true in Britain, where dramatic increases have been reported over the last 20 years.

EDIBLE FROG FACT FILE

This is a well-marked frog, usually marbled with fresh green and black on its upperparts. Many individuals show a pale dorsal stripe. The snout is fairly long and pointed, and the legs are proportionately long by frog standards.

● **NAMES**
Common name: edible frog
Scientific name: *Rana* kl. *esculenta*

● **HABITAT**
Weed-infested freshwater pools, canals, flooded gravel pits and lake margins

● **DISTRIBUTION**
Lowland areas in south-east England

● **STATUS**
Introduced and established

● **SIZE**
Length 8–12cm (3¼–4½in) – much larger than the common frog

● **KEY FEATURES**
Brown to olive-green upper body, usually with black spots and irregular bands, and a pale stripe down back; thighs marbled yellow and black; underside whitish with dark spots; vocal sacs of breeding males white when inflated

● **HABITS**
Basks on banks, often in groups; males very vocal

● **VOICE**
Loud, staccato 'keh keh kehkeh ...' mating calls; other calls quieter

● **FOOD**
Mainly invertebrates

● **BREEDING**
Lays eggs in mid-May to June; froglets leave water in midsummer

Distribution map key

■ Present all year round

□ Not present

EDIBLE, MARSH AND POOL FROGS

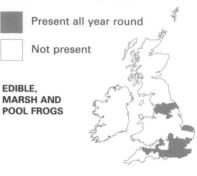

The brown or green colour looks brighter in strong sunlight.

The bulging eyes on top of the head have round pupils.

The snout is rounded and more pointed than that of a common frog.

around 7°C (45°F), the frogs become active and emerge to sit in the sun. If a cold snap occurs, they retire to the water once more. In spring and summer, they spend time feeding in deeper water, but seek shallow pools that warm up on sunny days to start their courtship.

Edible frogs can be easily detected in the mating season by the loud chorus of staccato calls made by the males to attract females. If they can be observed, the yellowish head and inflated cheek pouches of the calling males are good identification features.

The males serenade the females before actively seeking a mate. Egg-laying and fertilisation usually occur in weed-infested pools about 15cm (6in) deep, and take place in earnest only when the water temperature is around 18°C (64°F). A whole colony generally spawns at the same time, often over a few days, and the breeding frenzy continues throughout the day. Once darkness falls, the frogs retire to deeper water for the night and the colony falls silent. After spawning, the colony disperses and the adults take no further part in the care of their young.

The egg masses float near the surface where they are warmed by the summer

An edible frog tadpole is robust by the standards of other larval amphibians. It progresses along similar lines to its cousins, but the legs develop fully before the tail is reabsorbed.

sun. The tiny, black tadpoles that emerge are indistinguishable from those of related species. They feed on algae at first, then graduate to larger plants, debris on the pool bed and any waste matter they can find. Metamorphosis into tiny frogs takes place after a few weeks, depending on temperature and food supplies. The froglets stay fairly close to the breeding pools, unlike the young of common frogs, which disperse as soon as they leave the water.

With the onset of the first frosts of autumn, those tiny frogs that have survived the attacks of birds, snakes and pike – and larger frogs – join the adults from the previous year to seek out safe hibernation sites on the bottom of muddy pools. They remain there in a torpid state until warmer weather returns in the spring. The males may be mature enough to breed in their first year, but the females do not usually start breeding until they are two years old.

WILDLIFE WATCH

Where can I see edible frogs?

● Edible frogs favour warm conditions, so wait until sunny weather prevails in May or June before searching for them in ditches and streams.

● Listen for the loud chorus of calls in late spring, or for the 'plop' as frogs disturbed by your approach jump into the water.

● Approach the water carefully – edible frogs are easily frightened. Try using binoculars to watch the frogs from a distance without scaring them.

Recognising dragonflies

More than 20 species of dragonfly are on the wing near lakes, ponds and streams in the summer. Swift and efficient hunters, they tirelessly patrol their territories in search of insect prey.

Dragonflies, especially males, are among the most brilliantly coloured creatures to be found in the British Isles. Although often large and impressive in appearance, these insects are completely harmless, despite their old country name of 'horse-stingers'.

However, dragonflies are capable of reducing their insect prey to shreds in just a few seconds with their fearsome jaws. The victim is scooped up – the dragonfly's spiny legs forming a cage – and often chewed to pieces in flight, with rejected legs and wing cases scattered on the ground below.

Female and immature male broad-bodied chasers have stout, flattened abdomens, marked with yellow and brown. Mature males have a blue abdomen.

Dragonflies can identify their insect prey from great distances thanks to superb eyesight. In most native species, the huge, bulbous eyes – the largest of any insect – meet at the top of the head, and this gives them a wide field of vision.

Remarkably efficient in flight, with an extraordinary ability to fly sideways and backwards and to make instant switches of direction, the dragonfly's hunting is further aided by its ability to accelerate at an amazing rate.

WILDLIFE WATCH

Where can I see dragonflies?

● Dragonflies commonly visit garden ponds, and breed in ponds, lakes, canals, flooded gravel pits and slow-moving rivers and streams.

● The Norfolk Broads attract many species, but not the golden-ringed dragonfly.

● The gravel pits in the Cotswold Water Park are a superb dragonfly habitat.

● The Lake District and the dunes of the north-west coast provide rich breeding grounds and support some rare species.

● Wales is a stronghold of the golden-ringed dragonfly and keeled skimmer, plus some rare species. Kenfig National Nature Reserve and the Gwent Levels have excellent sites. The Dee, Severn, Wye, Tywi and Teifi are nationally important for the club-tailed dragonfly.

● In Scotland, Glen Affric and Loch Maree are home to the azure hawker as well as several rare species.

● In Ireland, the best location to see dragonflies is the Killarney National Park.

● In south-west England, Bodmin Moor, Dartmoor and the Somerset Levels have many dragonfly sites.

● The heathlands in Dorset, the New Forest and Surrey are prime dragonfly country, and attract rare species as well as the common ones.

EASY GUIDE TO SPOTTING DRAGONFLIES

WHAT ARE DRAGONFLIES?

● Dragonflies and damselflies belong to an insect order called Odonata, comprising approximately 5300 species worldwide. Of these, just over half are dragonflies, which belong to the suborder Anisoptera.

● Britain is home to 23 species of dragonfly. In most years, several more species arrive from the Continent – or even occasionally from the USA – but do not breed.

● Dragonfly nymphs (larvae) are a drab, brownish colour. They live in water for two years, preying on aquatic creatures such as tadpoles before developing, without a pupal stage, into the adult form.

● Dragonflies and damselflies have four densely veined wings, which beat independently of each other.

● When at rest, dragonflies hold their wings outwards; most damselflies fold them lengthwise along their bodies. Dragonflies have relatively stout bodies and large eyes that meet on top of the head; damselflies are smaller and slimmer, and their eyes do not meet on top.

Dragonflies have two feeding techniques – hawkers patrol their territory; chasers cling to plants and occasionally dart at passing prey.

Distribution map key
Present / Not present

AZURE HAWKER *Aeshna caerulea*

One of the world's most beautiful insects, the male is a spectacular sky blue and has an enamelled appearance. The female looks much like the female common hawker, but has no markings on top of the thorax (the part of an insect that lies between head and abdomen). The spots on the female's abdomen may be either yellow or pale blue.

Azure hawkers can be seen patrolling swampy moorland pools and damp Highland woods.

● SIZE
Length 62mm (2½in), wingspan 84mm (3¼in)

● HABITAT
Small, peaty bog-pools with abundant *Sphagnum* mosses, for nymphs; open moorland and damp, ancient woodlands

● DISTRIBUTION
Mainly in the Highlands of Scotland, especially Inverness; also in south-west Scotland

● FLIGHT SEASON
Late May–early August

COMMON HAWKER *Aeshna juncea*

Despite its name, this species is absent over much of lowland Britain. The male is similar to the azure hawker but a duller blue, and it has two yellowish stripes on the thorax. In the female, these are reduced to two dots. Most females are brown and yellow, but some are pale green or – in Scotland – pale blue.

Sit beside a pond and you may be lucky enough to see a female common hawker laying her eggs in the aquatic vegetation.

● SIZE
Length 74mm (3in), wingspan 95mm (3¾in)

● HABITAT
Heathland and moorland. Prefers acidic pools and lakes for breeding; will sometimes use neutral waters

● DISTRIBUTION
Common in north and west; absent from much of eastern and southern England

● FLIGHT SEASON
July–October; sometimes June–early November

MIGRANT HAWKER *Aeshna mixta*

This is the smallest of the hawkers that occur in southern England. A yellow triangle on the abdomen distinguishes both sexes from the common hawker, and two yellow dots on top of the thorax replace the broad green or yellow bands found on the southern hawker. Males are blue; females resemble the female common hawker.

Migrant hawker populations are augmented by an influx from the Continent in late summer.

● SIZE
Length 63mm (2½in), wingspan 87mm (3½in)

● HABITAT
Lowland lakes, ponds, canals and gravel pits; often found far from water

● DISTRIBUTION
South Wales, southern and central England; spreading north and west from colonisation in south-east in 1940s

● FLIGHT SEASON
Late July–October or November

SOUTHERN HAWKER *Aeshna cyanea*

The southern hawker is easily differentiated from other hawkers by the broad green bands on top of the thorax. The male is the only hawker that is spotted with green and blue. The similar hairy dragonfly is smaller, flies earlier – in May and June – and has no green markings on its abdomen.

A pair of lime green stripes on the abdomen identify a southern hawker at rest.

- **SIZE**
  Length 70mm (2¾in), wingspan 98mm (3⅞in)

- **HABITAT**
  Lakes and ponds in or near woodland; often lays eggs in garden ponds; adults commonly seen along woodland rides

- **DISTRIBUTION**
  Wales and England to Cumbria and Durham; isolated populations in Scotland; virtually absent from Ireland

- **FLIGHT SEASON**
  July–early October

BROWN HAWKER *Aeshna grandis*

This is the only large brown hawker that is common throughout much of England. The similar Norfolk hawker, distinguished by a yellow triangle on its abdomen, is restricted to a few sites in East Anglia. Male brown hawkers have blue spots along the sides of the abdomen and bluish eyes. The wings are heavily tinted, unlike those of the Norfolk hawker, which are clear.

Cool, dull days are good for observing hawkers at rest. The brown hawker is easily identified by its distinctive bronze-coloured wings.

- **SIZE**
  Length 73mm (3in), wingspan 102mm (4in)

- **HABITAT**
  Lowland ponds, lakes, gravel pits, garden ponds, canals and slow-moving rivers; males hunt far from water

- **DISTRIBUTION**
  As far north as Lancashire and Yorkshire; absent from south-west England and west Wales; Ireland except in south

- **FLIGHT SEASON**
  June–October

EMPEROR DRAGONFLY *Anax imperator*

Male emperors can often be seen hawking across lakes and ponds, sometimes at speeds of up to 18mph (30km/h). The male's abdomen is bright blue with a black line down the centre, and its thorax is green. The female is apple green all over, except for a slightly broader black line down the centre of the abdomen.

With the largest wingspan of any British dragonfly, the emperor is also striking for its coloration.

- **SIZE**
  Length 78mm (3⅛in), wingspan 107mm (4⅛in)

- **HABITAT**
  Ponds, lakes, garden ponds with abundant vegetation; frequently disappears after a year or two

- **DISTRIBUTION**
  South of a line from Blackpool to Hull; absent from north-west Wales

- **FLIGHT SEASON**
  Early June–late August, exceptionally into September

CLUB-TAILED DRAGONFLY *Gomphus vulgatissimus*

The sexes are very similar, but males become pale green on top as they mature, although the spots along the sides of the abdomen near its tip remain yellow. The female has a less waisted abdomen than the male. The club shape of the tip of the abdomen is more pronounced than in other British species.

The only British species with widely separated eyes, the club-tailed has bold yellow markings when newly emerged.

- **SIZE**
  Length 50mm (2in), wingspan 64mm (2½in)

- **HABITAT**
  Slow-moving rivers with silted bottoms, for nymphs, and bankside trees for emerging adults

- **DISTRIBUTION**
  Mainly on the Severn and Thames and some of their tributaries; also on the Arun in Sussex

- **FLIGHT SEASON**
  Early May–late June

GOLDEN-RINGED DRAGONFLY *Cordulegaster boltonii*

Easy to identify from its black abdomen ringed with yellow, this dragonfly's narrow, greenish eyes only just meet in a point on top of the head. The male has a more club-shaped abdomen than the female, which is the longest bodied of all British dragonflies because of its long ovipositor (egg-laying organ).

One of the largest of British dragonflies, the male golden-ringed can be seen hunting throughout its habitat.

● SIZE
Length male 74mm (3in), female 84mm (3¼in), wingspan 102mm (4in)

● HABITAT
Moorland and heathland streams; often found in fields, gardens and woodland edges

● DISTRIBUTION
Mainly north and west; absent from most of central and eastern England, and Ireland

● FLIGHT SEASON
End May–early September

FOUR-SPOTTED CHASER *Libellula quadrimaculata*

Unlike other chasers, the male and female four-spotted chaser are virtually identical – dark brown with black-tipped, narrowly tapered abdomens with yellow spots along the sides. Their wing-bases are blackish brown, as they are in other chaser species, with a dark brown spot on the leading edge of each wing.

Small and brown coloured, the four-spotted chaser may be difficult to see, clinging to vegetation ready to dart at passing prey.

● SIZE
Length 43mm (1¾in), wingspan 76mm (3in)

● HABITAT
Lakes, canals, garden ponds and gravel pits in lowland areas, and acidic moorland pools; females spend much time away from water

● DISTRIBUTION
Most of the British Isles; absent from part of south and central Wales

● FLIGHT SEASON
Late May–mid-August

BROAD-BODIED CHASER *Libellula depressa*

Both male and female broad-bodied chasers have dark wing-bases and are yellowish brown when young. The female darkens with age, while the male gradually becomes a bright, powdery blue. Mature males and females have a row of bright yellow spots down the sides of the abdomen. The male of the very similar scarce chaser has a narrower abdomen with a black tip.

The broad, flattened abdomen of this species is its most obvious identification feature.

● SIZE
Length 44mm (1¾in), wingspan 76mm (3in)

● HABITAT
Any kind of still water, but prefers smallish ponds, often colonising new bodies of water very quickly

● DISTRIBUTION
South of a line from Liverpool to the Wash; absent from mountains of north Wales and all of Ireland

● FLIGHT SEASON
Mid-May–early August

BLACK-TAILED SKIMMER *Orthetrum cancellatum*

The clear wings and black tip to the male's abdomen identify this species. It is larger than chasers and has a slimmer body. Immatures of both sexes are yellowish with two black lines down the top of the abdomen, which fade with age. The females become dark brown, and the males suffused with pale blue.

Males especially spend much time basking on bare ground, returning to a favoured spot in between bouts of skimming flight.

● SIZE
Length 50mm (2in), wingspan 78mm (3⅛in)

● HABITAT
Lakes, ponds, gravel pits and small rivers, with bare ground around margins

● DISTRIBUTION
Mainly south of a line from Grimsby to Swansea, and in central Ireland; expanding due to flooding of gravel pits

● FLIGHT SEASON
Late May–early August

KEELED SKIMMER · *Orthetrum coerulescens*

Apart from not having a black tail, this species is very similar to the black-tailed skimmer. Immature keeled skimmers are yellow or light brown. Mature females darken, while males become a powdery blue. The female resembles a common darter, but has two pale stripes on the thorax. The scarce chaser is similar, but has dark wing-bases and the male has a black tail.

An unusual characteristic of the keeled skimmer is that it rests with its wings angled forward.

● **SIZE**
Length 42mm (1¾in), wingspan 60mm (2⅜in)

● **HABITAT**
Acidic streams and bog-pools on peaty heaths and moors; adults do not stray far from breeding areas

● **DISTRIBUTION**
Scattered throughout Britain; common in Cornwall; absent from large areas of Midlands and most of eastern Britain

● **FLIGHT SEASON**
Early June–late August

COMMON DARTER · *Sympetrum striolatum*

Immatures are yellowish or pale brown. Mature females are slightly darker and have black markings on the sides of the abdomen; mature males are reddish orange. The abdomen is fairly slender and the legs are black with pale yellow stripes. The similar Highland darter seems to be a slightly darker northern form of this species, with more black on its underside.

As summer progresses, common darters spend an increasing amount of time sunbathing or resting on tree bark or the ground.

● **SIZE**
Length 37mm (1½in), wingspan 57mm (2¼in)

● **HABITAT**
Still or slow-moving water ranging from small garden ponds to large lakes; also rivers, canals, ditches and even slightly brackish water, shaded or unshaded

● **DISTRIBUTION**
Common throughout much of the British Isles

● **FLIGHT SEASON**
June–October, often into November or, rarely, December

RUDDY DARTER · *Sympetrum sanguineum*

The male ruddy darter has a blood-red abdomen, which is much brighter than the common darter's, and a distinctly narrow waist. The female resembles the female common darter. Both sexes have all-black legs with no yellow stripes, and are smaller than the common darter. Males often perch near still water.

The male ruddy darter's narrow waist makes the tip of the abdomen appear club-shaped.

● **SIZE**
Length 34mm (1⅜in), wingspan 55mm (2¼in)

● **HABITAT**
Semishaded ponds, lakes, canals and slow-moving streams with abundant vegetation

● **DISTRIBUTION**
Lowland areas of England south of a line from Preston to Hull and far south of Wales; rare in south-west; common in Ireland

● **FLIGHT SEASON**
July–late September

BLACK DARTER · *Sympetrum danae*

The species is named after the mature male, which is more or less completely black and has a waisted abdomen. Females and immature males are yellowish and could be mistaken for common or ruddy darters were it not for the presence of a black triangle on the thorax.

Britain's smallest dragonfly, the black darter may be identified by its small size alone.

● **SIZE**
Length 32mm (1¼in), wingspan 47mm (2in)

● **HABITAT**
Acidic pools on heaths and moors, and bogs, with plenty of floating or emergent vegetation

● **DISTRIBUTION**
Mainly west and north of England; absent from most of Midlands and from eastern England south of north Norfolk

● **FLIGHT SEASON**
July–October

Swarms of midges

It is easy to curse the midge when a summer evening stroll by a river or lake side is ruined by their biting swarms, but countless creatures depend on these tiny insects for food – and by no means all midges bite.

Midges is a handy catch-all name for a mixed bag of two-winged flies – including mosquitoes, blackflies and gnats – that gather in frenzied swarms to mate on sultry summer evenings. To confuse things further, there are a number of different flies that are actually called midges. Some species bite; others do not.

The most-maligned midge is the non-biting chironomid midge. There are more than 450 species breeding in Britain, and they occur in vast numbers. The flying adults may be pests, but their aquatic larvae play an important part in sustaining freshwater communities. Some larvae are predatory, but many others eat microscopic plants and help to recycle waste by eating tiny particles of decaying plants and animals known collectively as organic detritus.

Chironomid larvae often live in tubes deep in the mud at the bottom of ponds, where there is very little dissolved oxygen. To improve their oxygen supply, these larvae pump water through their burrows. Other larvae, known as bloodworms, have the red pigment called haemoglobin in their bodies, which assists them in storing oxygen. You can easily find bloodworms by sifting through the mud at the bottom of a garden pond. Many goldfish, carp and bream spend their lives doing just that – digging into pond, lake and river beds in search of midge larvae to eat. Fish are so keen to find as many bloodworms as possible that the whole bottom of a lake may be churned over several times during the course of a year.

Life for the chironomid midge is fraught with dangers. As a larva, it is hunted by leeches and flatworms, and

◄ Bloodworms are the aquatic larvae of some non-biting chironomid midges. By storing oxygen in their red pigment, they can survive in stagnant mud.

▼ This adult female *Chironomus plumosus* midge has plain antennae and long wings. The male has feathery antennae and short wings.

MOSQUITOES

There are around 30 British mosquito species breeding in still or stagnant pools and they behave very like midges. The larvae are the little black 'commas' you see wriggling in garden water butts and ponds. They filter tiny food particles out of the water and take in air at the surface through a tube. Adults use their piercing mouthparts to suck juices from flowers and fruits. Females require a meal of blood before they can produce eggs. To get this, some bite birds or animals; others bite humans – itchy reactions to mosquito bites can make life a misery in summer. But at least in Britain, a bite does not carry the risk of diseases such as malaria and yellow fever, as it does in the tropics.

sifted from the sediment by bottom-feeding fishes and diving ducks, such as pochard and tufted ducks. When the surviving larvae pupate and rise slowly to the surface, they fall prey to mid-water feeding fish such as perch and trout.

Once at the surface, adult midges must emerge and dry their wings before they can fly away. At this stage, they make easy pickings for more fish and for ducklings. Then, as they fly off, they are snapped up by swallows, martins and swifts. Midges are not even safe after dark, when bats, such as the pipistrelle, swoop over lakes and ponds, catching them by the dozen.

It is amazing that these tiny flies form the staple diet of so many aquatic and waterside animals and still survive in sufficient numbers to create a humming mist beside the water. Nonetheless, there are always thousands of larvae per square metre of lake bed preparing to replenish the swarm.

The ones that bite

Chironomids are joined in midge swarms by the far more pesky ceratopogonids – the biting midges. As small eel-like larvae, biting midges live in river, lake and pool sediments eating detritus. The adults may be only a millimetre long, which helps to explain their American nickname of 'no-see ums'. You are certainly likely to feel

Sitting on a leaf like this, the adult male chironomid is resting rather than feeding. In any case, he has very weak mouth parts and many never feed at all.

the attentions of the females, however, because what they lack in size they more than make up for with their bite. Like mosquitoes, the female biting midge needs to suck a blood meal to kick-start her egg production.

The most famous of these female biting midges are the notorious Scottish Highland midges, but you can also suffer their attentions in the hills of Northumberland and elsewhere. They thrive in their millions in small stagnant peaty pools, emerging as adults to target unfortunate tourists, especially on sultry summer evenings. Some people have a marked allergic reaction to midge bites, developing large, itchy, red bumps, which may last for several days and turn an idyllic holiday into an unforgettable experience – for all the wrong reasons. The moral of this tale is never go north in summer without your insect repellent.

See-through larvae

Phantom midges are better known as gnats. They are non-biting flies that live as larvae in lakes, where they are a favourite prey of fish. The larvae do their best to avoid being eaten by having almost perfectly transparent bodies and by lying in muddy sediments during the day. After dusk, they use little air-filled buoyancy organs to rise up into the upper water layers where they hunt water fleas.

The Dixidae is another family of flies in which the adults look like many other small, dark, midge-like flies. There are 14 British species, all of which are noteworthy because their larvae often crawl on the surface of the water filtering out tiny edible particles.

The River Stour which flows through Blandford Forum in Dorset is home to the dreaded 'Blandford fly', a species of blackfly. As with all midge-like biters, this

Having spent two to three years as a larva, an adult midge only lives for a few hours – or days at the most. Its sole aim is to mate and, if it is a female, to lay eggs.

fly's mouth parts are superbly adapted to puncture even thick, hard skin. Allergic reactions to Blandford fly bites produce sore, itchy bumps.

Blackfly larvae live in running waters. They attach themselves to submerged weeds and filter food particles from the passing water. After emerging from the water as adults, female blackflies bite livestock and people indiscriminately in order to obtain their vital blood meal.

As they emerge from the water as adults, midges mate in vast swarms that dance in the air.

WILDLIFE WATCH

Where can I go to see midges?

● Usually the question is 'Where can I go to get away from swarms of midges?' to which the answer is: 'Avoid freshwater.' By lakes or rivers, you can catch a good assortment of midges in a butterfly net and identify them with a hand lens.

● Midge larvae are easier to observe at close quarters than the adults. Search for them at the bottom of the pond and put them in a glass jar to observe their behaviour.

Water-crowfoots: floating carpets

The masses of delicate flowers that cover the surface of clear streams, ponds, sometimes even ditches, all belong to an adaptable family of aquatic buttercup.

Water-crowfoots, or water buttercups as they are sometimes known, are a group of aquatic buttercups. Unlike yellow-flowered buttercups, water-crowfoots have white and yellow flowers.

The scientific name for all buttercups is *Ranunculus*. This means 'little frog' in Latin and emphasises that these plants have a preference for moist habitats. The ten species of water-crowfoot that are native to Britain and Ireland are all very similar and can cross-breed with one another, but not with a yellow buttercup.

Water-crowfoots are usually perennial, but a few are annual or biennial. The stems are flexible and trail in the water. The flowers are carried slightly above the water surface and, not surprisingly,

The white flowers of pond water-crowfoot may often be seen on the upper reaches of chalk streams.

have the typical structure of the buttercup: the central mass of stigmas (the part that receives pollen) is surrounded by yellow anthers (containing pollen grains) and a ring of petals that are white with yellow bases. The fruit is a tight head of single-seeds, each resembling a tiny nut.

Flowering takes place in spring and summer, though often for a relatively short period. During this time, insects visit the flowers to pollinate them just as if the plants were growing on land.

Choice of leaves

Water-crowfoots are unusual in having two sorts of leaf – flat ones that float on the surface or rise out of the water, and submerged leaves that are divided into many long, slender segments. Two native species have only floating or aerial leaves, and three have only submerged leaves. The other five species have a mixture of both.

These different leaf types of the crowfoots have resulted from individual species adapting to different environments. Ivy-leaved water-crowfoot, for example, grows mainly on damp mud and is unable to produce submerged leaves. River water-crowfoot on the other hand, which produces only submerged leaves, occurs in deep, fast-flowing water, where floating leaves would be damaged or swept away.

As its name suggests, common water-crowfoot is the most abundant and widespread of this prolific family. It covers shallow waters with a profusion of pale flowers.

Common water-crowfoot produces both types of leaf, enabling it to tolerate a variety of water levels, even occasional droughts when small ponds and streams dry up. Such flexibility makes it the most widespread and common of all water-crowfoots.

Although water-crowfoots are still widespread, water pollution, the drainage of wetlands and the silting-up of small ponds mean there are fewer places for them to grow these days. Only one species, the three-lobed water-crowfoot, is scarce throughout the British Isles. It grows in temporary pools and damp, rutted tracks on heaths and commons in the west, especially on the Lizard Peninsula in Cornwall. At one time, it was thought that the three-lobed water-crowfoot had been displaced in southern England by a hybrid derived from cross-breeding between three-lobed and round-leaved water-crowfoots. However, what were believed to be old specimens of three-lobed water-crowfoot from streams in the New Forest turned out to be early examples of the hybrid that still grows there.

WATER-CROWFOOT FACT FILE

● **Common water-crowfoot**
Ranunculus aquatilis
Habitat and distribution
Widespread and sometimes common in clear, nutrient-rich, shallow streams, ponds and ditches
Size Stems up to 50cm (20in) long
Key features
Annual or perennial; submerged leaves with thread-like segments; floating leaves long-stalked, semicircular or circular, flat blade divided into 3–7 toothed lobes; flowers white, 12–18mm (½–¾in) across, petals longer than spreading sepals; fruits downy, on stalks shorter than adjacent leaf
Flowering time
May–July

● **Pond water-crowfoot**
Ranunculus peltatus
Habitat and distribution
Widespread and common in nutrient-rich streams, ponds and shallow lakes
Size Stems up to 100cm (3ft 3in) long
Key features
Similar to *R. aquatilis*, but leaves less sharply toothed; flowers white, 15–20mm (⅝–¾in) across; fruit-stalks longer than adjacent leaf
Flowering time
May–August

● **Brackish water-crowfoot**
Ranunculus baudotii
Habitat and distribution
Brackish, nutrient-rich pools and ditches often near sea, perhaps declining
Size Stems 10–30cm (4–12in) long

Key features
Annual or perennial; submerged leaves yellowish green with thread-like segments; floating leaves, deeply divided into 3 lobes, flat bladed, sometimes absent; flowers white, 12–18mm (½–¾in) across, petals longer than bent-back, blue-tipped sepals; fruits hairless, on stalks longer than adjacent leaf
Flowering time
May–September

● **Three-lobed water-crowfoot**
Ranunculus tripartitus
Habitat and distribution
Rare in temporary pools, ponds, ditches and ruts on lime-poor soils, mainly in west Wales and Cornwall; also west Cork
Size Stems up to 40cm (16in) long
Key features
Annual or perennial; submerged leaves yellowish green with thread-like segments; floating leaves flat bladed, deeply divided into 3 or 5 wedge-shaped, bluntly toothed lobes; flowers white, 3–10mm (⅛–½in) across, petals up to twice as long as bent-back, blue-tipped sepals; fruits hairless
Flowering time
March–June

● **Stream water-crowfoot**
Ranunculus penicillatus
Habitat and distribution
Widespread and often common in nutrient-rich, fast-flowing rivers and streams, mainly over limestone, not in parts of north
Size Stems 100–200cm (3ft 3in–6ft 6in) long
Key features
Similar to pond water-crowfoot, but more robust; floating leaves sometimes absent, submerged leaves long and limp
Flowering time
June–July

WILDLIFE WATCH

Where do water-crowfoots grow?

● Water-crowfoots form floating mats of vegetation on a range of still to fast-flowing waters in rivers, streams, shallow lakes, ponds, drainage dykes and temporary pools – even on disturbed, damp mud. They flourish especially well in the clear, unpolluted waters of chalk streams, which are rich in nutrients.

Common water-crowfoot
Ranunculus aquatilis

Pond water-crowfoot
Ranunculus peltatus

Brackish water-crowfoot
Ranunculus baudotii

Three-lobed water-crowfoot
Ranunculus tripartitus

Stream water-crowfoot
Ranunculus penicillatus

WATER-CROWFOOT FACT FILE

● Ivy-leaved water-crowfoot
Ranunculus hederaceus
Habitat and distribution
Widespread and common on bare mud, in temporary pools and damp ruts; less frequent in north
Size Stems 10–40cm (4–16in) long
Key features
Annual or perennial with creeping stems; leaves long-stalked, flat bladed, divided into 5 short, rounded lobes, widest near base; flowers white, 3–6mm (⅛–¼in) across, petals as long as spreading sepals; fruits hairless
Flowering time
April–September

● Round-leaved water-crowfoot
Ranunculus omiophyllus
Habitat and distribution
Lime-poor, slow-moving streams, shallow pools and ditches, mainly in southern and western Britain and southern Ireland
Size Stems 10–40cm (4–16in) long
Key features
Similar to ivy-leaved crowfoot, but annual or biennial; leaves flat bladed, deeply divided into 5 lobes, widest above base; flowers white, 8–12mm (⅜–½in) across, petals at least twice as long as bent-back sepals
Flowering time
April–August

● River water-crowfoot
Ranunculus fluitans
Habitat and distribution
Fast-flowing rivers, mainly in south and east, north to central Scotland, also County Antrim in Ireland; rare in south-west England and Wales
Size Stems 1–6m (3ft 3in–20ft) long

Key features
Perennial; leaves up to 50cm (20in) long, with thread-like segments, all submerged; flowers white, 20–30mm (¾–1¼in) across, petals longer than spreading sepals; fruits hairy when young
Flowering time June–August

● Fan-leaved water-crowfoot
Ranunculus circinatus
Habitat and distribution
Lakes, rivers, canals and ditches north to southern Scotland; rare north of the Midlands and in Ireland
Size Stems up to 100cm (3ft 3in) long
Key features
Perennial; leaves all submerged, short, with thread-like segments spreading in flat circle; flowers white, 8–18mm (⅜–¾in) across, petals scarcely touch one another; fruits hairy when young
Flowering time
May–August

● Thread-leaved water-crowfoot
Ranunculus trichophyllus
Habitat and distribution
Widespread in shallow, still or slow-flowing waters, or on wet mud; most in south and east
Size: Stems up to 100cm (3ft 3in) long
Key features
Annual or perennial; rather slender; submerged leaves short, with thread-like segments spreading in bushy mass; flowers white, 5–10mm (¼–½in) across, petals about as long as spreading sepals; fruits downy when young
Flowering time
April–July

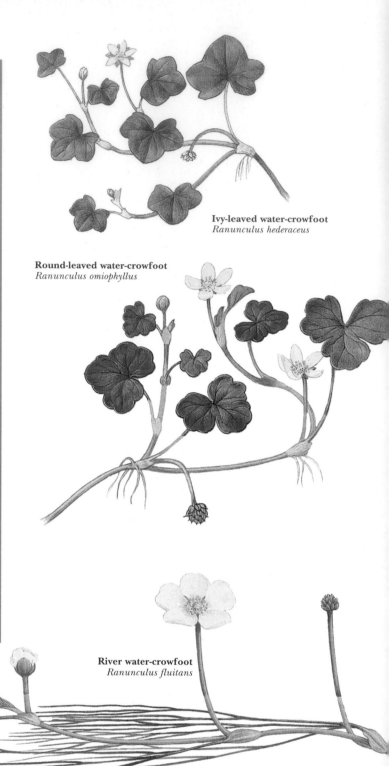

Ivy-leaved water-crowfoot
Ranunculus hederaceus

Round-leaved water-crowfoot
Ranunculus omiophyllus

River water-crowfoot
Ranunculus fluitans

Fan-leaved water-crowfoot
Ranunculus circinatus

Thread-leaved water-crowfoot
Ranunculus trichophyllus

Coast watch

- Recognising dolphins
- Following the pilot whale
- Recognising terns
- The cormorant
- Recognising crabs
- The starfish
- Recognising seashells
- Sponges – living sieves
- Recognising seaweeds
- Sea-lavender and thrift

Recognising dolphins

Dolphins and porpoises look very much alike, especially if you catch only a fleeting glimpse. However, it is possible to identify different species by the shapes of their heads and fins – and by how they behave in the water.

The sight of a dolphin, even the quick flash of a fin, usually creates a great deal of excitement among onlookers. Many people assume it must be an unusual event but, in fact, a total of 28 species of cetaceans – that is whales, dolphins and porpoises – have been recorded in British and Irish waters, and six of these are seen fairly often.

Dolphins and porpoises are smaller members of the order Cetacea, which comprises the great baleen whales and the toothed whales; dolphins and porpoises fall into the latter category.

The most frequently sighted cetacean is the common porpoise, which is found mainly in the waters around Scotland and along the western coast of Britain and Ireland. Despite the frequency of sightings, the common porpoise is actually a shy creature, and notoriously difficult to get close to.

The two dolphin species most often recorded by naturalists are the white-beaked dolphin and the bottle-nosed dolphin, followed by the common dolphin, the Atlantic white-sided dolphin and Risso's dolphin.

Watching from shore

Some areas of the coast, specifically Cornwall, Wales, western Ireland and Scotland, provide much better opportunities than others for watching dolphins. However, in summer at least, it is possible to see one or two species of dolphin off almost any part of the coastline.

Bottle-nosed dolphins are often found close to shore and provide the casual observer with the best opportunities of seeing one of these playful creatures. Small groups of resident and semiresident bottle-nosed dolphins have been identified in scattered areas around the coast. The striped dolphin is a rare visitor to our offshore waters and is not included in this identification guide.

While several species of dolphin can be seen from the shore, your chances increase the further you are from land. Ferries and similar vessels offer the possibility of a sighting when crossing the Irish Sea, the English Channel or even the Solent en route to the Isle of Wight.

In Scotland, cruises around the Hebrides, Orkney and Shetland offer opportunities to see Risso's dolphins as well as other cetacean species.

Cardigan Bay in Wales and the Moray Firth in Scotland are sites of resident bottle-nosed dolphin groups, and organised trips allow fairly close observation. Dolphins can be seen from the shore in some areas of the Moray Firth.

Vessels approaching dolphins should always adhere to a strict code of conduct – the vessel should travel on a parallel course to the dolphins and slow down so that the dolphins can approach if they wish.

When dolphins leap clear of the water, it gives you the chance to note the shape of the beak, the position of the dorsal fin and the colour on the flanks, which all help identification.

EASY GUIDE TO SPOTTING DOLPHINS

HOW CAN I IDENTIFY DOLPHINS AND PORPOISES?

● As with all animals, identification comes from observing and recording key features. Dolphins and porpoises are large mammals, but much of the body is hidden beneath the water, hindering efforts to identify them. Getting a good view depends on sea conditions, especially when watching from land.

● When a dolphin surfaces, the head is usually seen first, then the dorsal fin and the rest of the back before it submerges. The shape and position of the dorsal fin are good indications of the species' identity. A porpoise has a small triangular dorsal fin, whereas this fin is sickle-shaped in a dolphin.

● Dolphin and porpoise heads can be divided into three shapes – beaked, such as the bottle-nosed dolphin; rounded with no beak or forehead, such as the common porpoise; and blunt shaped with a forehead, such as the Risso's dolphin.

● Coloured markings and patterns on the flanks are important features to note.

For example, a pale grey or white patch is clearly visible behind the dorsal fin on the white-beaked dolphin. The common dolphin has a yellow patch running along the side of its body from the beak to below the dorsal fin, and the Atlantic white-sided dolphin has a yellow marking from behind its dorsal fin to its tail.

● If the dolphin leaps out of the water (a porpoise does this only rarely), some distinctive features will be exposed. Does it have a long beak, short beak or none at all?

● Bottle-nosed dolphins, common dolphins and white-beaked dolphins sometimes ride a vessel's bow wave, and it may be possible to get a clear view of identifying features.

● Dolphin skin is easily scarred, and cetacean biologists identify individual dolphins by the numerous nicks, cuts and marks on the dorsal fin and other parts of the body.

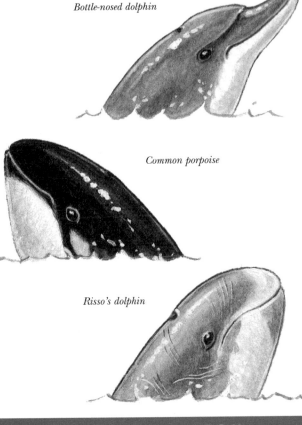

Bottle-nosed dolphin

Common porpoise

Risso's dolphin

HOW CAN I GET A CLOSER LOOK?

● Binoculars are an important tool for the dolphin watcher. The best magnification range is between 7x and 10x. The lower end of the range has good light gathering, which is useful when looking out to sea. It is best to scan the sea with the naked eye as well as through binoculars to prevent eye strain. Look for splashes or surface disturbance. Calm seas provide the prime conditions for observation.

● Telescopes can be useful when watching from the land. A 20x magnification is best; greater than this the view may

be too dim and the field of view too limiting. Cetaceans often surface and dive before you can get a good look at them. A camera or video camera can be a useful tool, allowing you to photograph the animals and look for identifiable features later.

The common dolphin often swims alongside ships and plays around boats. When it rides the bow wave or breaks the water's surface, you can get a clear view of its head, back and dorsal fin.

WILDLIFE WATCH

Where can I see dolphins and porpoises?

● Dolphins and porpoises are most commonly seen in the waters around Scotland and the western coast of Britain and Ireland, but dolphins especially may be seen along almost any part of the coastline. It is a matter of being in the right place at the right time. When watching from the shore, choose a high vantage point.

● Bottle-nosed dolphins can be observed in the Moray Firth in Scotland and Cardigan Bay in Wales. Boat trips are available in both locations during the summer, and there is an Information Centre at Cardigan Bay. A small group of bottle-nosed dolphins, among other species, is being studied off the coast of Durlston in Dorset. Sounds made by the dolphins and picked up by a hydrophone can be heard in the Durlston Country Park Centre.

● A sociable bottle-nosed dolphin called Fungi has lived in Dingle Bay in

Co. Kerry, Ireland, since 1987. Although completely wild, Fungi chooses to interact with humans. Visitors are taken by boat to see him, and may even don wetsuits to swim with him. Due to the increased awareness of dolphins' welfare needs, there are no longer any dolphinariums in Britain.

● The Sea Life Survey is a joint venture run by the World Wide Fund for Nature and the Marine Life Information Network. To find out more about it and to report sightings, telephone 0845 1210500 (www.marlin. ac.uk/sealifesurvey)

● The Sea Watch Foundation monitors the distribution and movements of cetaceans in British waters. It is interested in receiving details of any species sighted in Britain and in hearing from anyone who would like to take part. Contact Sea Watch on 01865 764794.

BOTTLE-NOSED DOLPHIN *Tursiops truncatus*

One of the most familiar of Britain's native dolphin, these creatures may be seen in some areas all year round, often in groups as this is a very sociable species. They sometimes appear in small numbers in unexpected places during the summer months. Bottle-nosed dolphins are naturally curious and may approach vessels and ride bow waves, leaping clear of the water.

● SIZE
Length 2–4m
(6ft 6in–13ft)

● BREEDING
Single calf; births peak in summer

● FOOD
A wide range of fish; squid; occasionally crustaceans

● HABITAT
Offshore and coastal water populations; can sometimes be seen from land

● DISTRIBUTION
Main concentrations along east coast of Scotland and south-west coast of England, Cardigan Bay and the Llŷn Peninsula in Wales, west coasts of Ireland and Cornwall; small semiresident groups in scattered locations around coast; summer inshore movements occur elsewhere. Only breeding sites in Britain are Cardigan Bay and the Moray Firth

● STATUS
One of the most frequently seen cetaceans; relatively abundant, particularly around Scotland and western coasts; apparently declining in south

Bottle-nosed dolphins have no colourful flank markings to help identification. However, the uniform grey colour, the big, sickle-shaped dorsal fin and short beak are distinctive.

Prominent sickle-shaped dorsal fin located centrally on back

Slate grey or brownish grey back with paler grey or brownish sides and a whitish underside

Short beak; lower jaw protrudes beyond upper jaw

COMMON DOLPHIN *Delphinus delphis*

This mainly open-water species is usually seen in small groups, but common dolphins may occasionally form large herds of several hundred individuals. The species is recorded all year round, but is more likely to be seen in coastal waters between July and October than at other times. It has a slender beak and a distinctive hourglass pattern of a yellowish colour with grey on its flanks.

● SIZE
Length 1.7–2.5m
(5ft 10in–8ft 2in)

● BREEDING
Birthing seasons not known for certain in British waters; June–September in North Atlantic

● FOOD
Fish and squid

● HABITAT
An open-water species but also ventures inshore; occasionally enters large rivers

● DISTRIBUTION
Common in western approach to English Channel; also occurs off western coasts of Britain and Ireland; widespread in the North Sea

● STATUS
Regularly seen from some coasts but mainly offshore; less common than name suggests

The common dolphin frequently breaks the water's surface, making its attractive markings easily visible. It is regularly observed riding the bow wave of vessels.

Sickle-shaped dorsal fin

Prominent slender beak

Yellowish or tan panel on forward flanks

Grey panel on flanks from below dorsal fin to tail

RISSO'S DOLPHIN *Grampus griseus*

A large, robust-bodied species resembling the pilot whale in shape, Risso's dolphin has a distinctive sickle-shaped dorsal fin, a rounded forehead and no beak. Young Risso's are dark grey, but become lighter with age. The bodies of all adult Risso's are crisscrossed with fine, white scratches.

● **SIZE**
Length 2.8–3.3m (9ft 2in–10ft 10in), occasionally up to 3.8m (12ft 6in)

● **BREEDING**
Not known in British waters; April–September in North Atlantic

● **FOOD**
Mainly squid and cuttlefish; some fish

● **HABITAT**
Not well known in British waters

● **DISTRIBUTION**
Western coast of Britain and Ireland, Irish Sea, Orkney and Shetland

● **STATUS**
Fairly common throughout range; usually seen as solitary individuals or in small groups

The crisscross marks on the Risso's body are scars from cuts inflicted by the teeth of others of its kind and, to a lesser extent, by its squid prey.

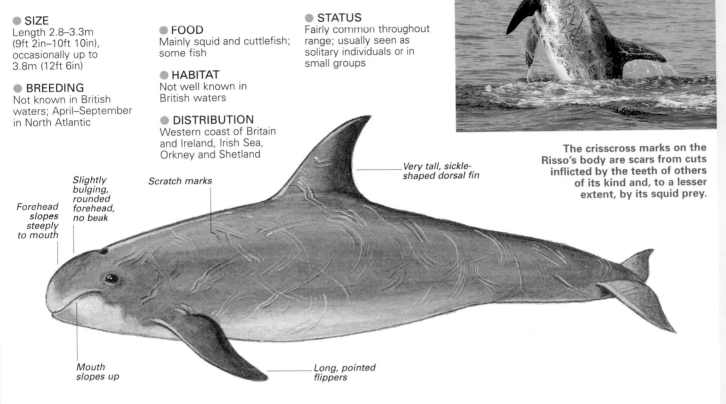

Forehead slopes steeply to mouth

Slightly bulging, rounded forehead, no beak

Scratch marks

Very tall, sickle-shaped dorsal fin

Mouth slopes up

Long, pointed flippers

WHITE-BEAKED DOLPHIN *Lagenorhynchus albirostrls*

As the name suggests, this dolphin usually – but not always – has a white beak. The beak is short and thick compared with that of the common dolphin. The pale grey or white markings on the side of the body are also a clue to identification. The dorsal fin is tall and sickle-shaped, especially in adult males.

● **SIZE**
Length 2.5–2.7m (8ft 2in–8ft 10in), occasionally up to 3m (9ft 10in)

● **BREEDING**
Most births thought to occur May–August

● **FOOD**
Fish, squid, octopus and some bottom-living crustaceans

● **HABITAT**
Often seen in coastal waters, usually in small groups; will associate with other species

● **DISTRIBUTION**
Northern and central North Sea and western coast of Britain and Ireland

● **STATUS**
Relatively common; one of the most frequently seen cetaceans; recorded all year round; most sightings in August

White-beaked dolphins are powerful, fast swimmers that sometimes perform acrobatics, especially when feeding. This species is solidly built, and is less sleek and streamlined than the common dolphin.

Short, often white beak

Sickle-shaped dorsal fin

White or pale grey markings along each side

ATLANTIC WHITE-SIDED DOLPHIN *Lagenorhynchus acutus*

Similar in size and shape to the white-beaked dolphin, this species can be distinguished by the yellow-ochre and white markings visible between the dorsal fin and tail when the dolphin surfaces to breathe. The black of the dolphin's back extends from the tail to the upper jaw of its short beak. This is a gregarious species and schools of up to 1000 have been recorded.

● **SIZE**
Length 2.5m (8ft 2in), sometimes up to 3m (9ft 10in)

● **BREEDING**
May–July in North Atlantic

● **FOOD**
Wide range of fish and squid; some crustaceans

● **HABITAT**
Mainly out at sea in deep waters; seasonal inshore movements occur late summer–autumn

● **DISTRIBUTION**
Mainly north-west of Britain and Ireland and northern areas of North Sea

● **STATUS**
Fairly common, particularly offshore; usually seen farther offshore than the white-beaked dolphin

Atlantic white-sided dolphins show their distinctive markings before diving. This species commonly breaks the water's surface, but is only occasionally observed bow riding.

Black, sickle-shaped dorsal fin

Short beak, black upper jaw

Yellow-ochre and white markings

COMMON OR HARBOUR PORPOISE *Phocoena phocoena*

This is the only porpoise found in British waters. A small, timid cetacean, it shows less of its body above water when surfacing to breathe than most dolphin species. The small, triangular dorsal fin and rounded snout are the best features for identification. The stubby body is dark grey on the back with paler sides. The common porpoise rarely leaps clear of the water.

● **SIZE**
Length 1.3–1.9m (4ft 4in–6ft 4in); females slightly larger than males

● **BREEDING**
Single calf born May–August

● **FOOD**
Fish, especially herring but also mackerel and whiting; cuttlefish

● **HABITAT**
Open sea and coastal waters, including estuaries and large rivers; seasonal inshore movements in summer and autumn

● **DISTRIBUTION**
Main concentrations in northern and western Britain; also seen along other areas of coast, usually in small groups of 2–4

● **STATUS**
The most commonly seen cetacean in British waters, due partly to inshore movements in spring

The rotund, torpedo-shaped body of the common porpoise is seen to best advantage from directly above. These porpoises seldom swim or dive in unison, as dolphins do.

Distinctive rounded head lacks prominent forehead; no beak

Short, triangular dorsal fin at mid-point of back

White belly; shades through dusky flanks to black back

Following the pilot whale

In the open sea, the pilot whale resembles a dark blunt torpedo ploughing steadily through the waves. Closer to shore, this animal's excellent navigational skills occasionally and mysteriously disappear, causing it to run aground.

As whales go, the pilot whale is a common species. Large numbers are frequently seen in British waters, especially off the coasts of the Hebridean islands, Shetland and Orkney. They also abound off the west coast of Ireland, but rarely venture into the North Sea and only occasionally into the English Channel, where they have been seen off the Kent and Sussex coasts. Sightings and reports of stranded whales increased steadily in the late 20th century, peaking in the 1970s and 1980s, but have become less frequent in recent years. The largest numbers are sighted offshore during the winter, between October and March, as the whales follow a seasonal migration route in pursuit of their food.

Pilot whales are usually slow swimmers, travelling at a leisurely 6mph (10km/h), but they can put on brief bursts of speed, going maybe four times faster. Their normal behaviour is placid and undemonstrative. They occasionally rest at the surface, and often adopt a 'bottling' posture where the body floats vertically. The whole front end, as far as the flippers, rises high above the surface so the animal can have a good look around – a habit known as 'spyhopping'. In captivity, pilot whales can be taught to leap from the water, but this behaviour is very rare among adults in the wild.

Herding instinct

Pilot whales live in social groups called herds, usually comprising a few dozen animals. Sometimes small groups join together, so that many whales are seen in the same area at once. The largest groups seen in British waters include 75 off north Wales in 1977 and 65 the previous year off

BLOWING

Pilot whales are mammals and need to breathe air regularly, so they have to surface periodically. On surfacing, they expel the stale air from their lungs through a single 'nostril', the blowhole, on the top of the head. Pilot whales surface to blow every two to ten minutes when they are cruising along. The domed head appears first, followed swiftly by an audible blast of spray and steamy air, which rises about 1.5m (5ft) above the water.

The curved dorsal fin then breaks the surface. Soon the whole flattish back is visible as the huge animal glides forwards. By comparison, most other small and medium-sized whales have a curved back and a distinctly pointed snout. A feeding dive often lasts five to ten minutes, sometimes longer, followed by a period of surface blows to get the breath back. Most dives are from 30–60m (100–200ft) but pilot whales can descend much deeper, to at least 600m (2000ft).

Apart from its almost entirely black skin and rounded head, the pilot whale's most distinctive feature is its unusually long flippers. These may be up to a fifth of the body length and have an obvious 'elbow'.

PROTECTED!

All species of whale are fully protected in British waters. Pilot whales are no longer hunted in Britain, but are still killed in the Faeroe Islands and other parts of the world.

PILOT WHALE FACT FILE

This jet-black, or dark grey, medium-sized whale has a long cylindrical body with a small, hooked dorsal fin a little in front of the midpoint on its straight back and very long, slender flippers positioned close to the head.

● **NAMES**
Common name: long-finned pilot whale
Scientific name: *Globiocephala melas*

● **HABITAT**
Coastal waters and open sea; sometimes gets stranded in shallow sandy bays and on muddy shores

● **DISTRIBUTION**
Mainly off northern and western coasts, especially off Scotland, also west of Ireland and tip of Cornwall

● **STATUS**
One of the most commonly seen whales in British waters, also one of the most frequently stranded species

● **SIZE**
Male length 5.5m (18ft), but up to 6.3m (21ft) or more; female length usually 4.6m (15ft); weight 1–3.5 tonnes; male generally larger than female, although a heavily pregnant female can weigh 5 tonnes

● **KEY FEATURES**
Mainly black with a paler underside, including pale greyish patch on the throat; long, straight back and long

flippers; male's dorsal fin usually more bulbous and curved backwards, with deeper concave trailing edge and longer base than female's; tail flukes have distinct notch in centre; each pilot whale acquires individual scars and nicks as it gets older

● **HABITS**
Gregarious, lives in social groups (herds)

● **FOOD**
Mostly squid and cuttlefish, but also some fish

● **BREEDING**
Any time; females start breeding at about 6 years old and males at 12; single births

● **YOUNG**
Similar to adult but develop colour and shape of fin with increasing age

Pilot whales have between 32 and 48 peg-like teeth for seizing their prey divided between the upper and lower jaws. The gums are as black as its body, but the tongue is pale pink.

The blunt, bulbous head of the pilot whale is quite different from the pointed snout of dolphins.

The dorsal fin is much nearer the head than in many other whale species. It is steeply curved backwards, but both curvature and shape depend on the sex of the whale and change with age.

The skin is smooth and soft, like a hard-boiled egg without its shell. Water flows past with little resistance, so the whale can swim along almost effortlessly.

The flippers are slender, with a distinct bend, especially in older individuals, and positioned close to the head.

Females have their mammary glands withdrawn into slits in the belly in order not to spoil the fine streamlining of the body.

Distribution map key

■ Present all year round

□ Not present

Whales sometimes become trapped in shallow water, leaving them beached and helpless when the tide goes out. They can die within hours unless rescued and refloated.

As long ago as the 14th century, legislation was passed making stranded whales the property of the sovereign. Nowadays, this royal right has been waived in favour of local authorities, animal welfare agencies and museums.

Nevertheless, for centuries it has been the quaint responsibility of Customs Officers to report all stranded whales to the Official Receiver of Wrecks who, since the early years of the 20th century, has been required to report

such incidents to the Natural History Museum in London. According to official documents, on average 150 whales were stranded each year throughout the 19th century, many of which were pilot whales. In all 140 strandings involving pilot whales were reported between 1913 and 1978.

Many strandings of single pilot whales have been reported on the south and west coasts, but the majority of these involved animals that had been caught in fishing nets and drifted ashore already dead.

The greatest mystery surrounds mass strandings, such as the 50 pilot whales that came ashore at Penzance in 1911 or even more inexplicably, the 30 pilot

whales that died in The Wash in 1982 – such whales are rarely found in the North Sea.

In such cases, scores of whales arrive in a shallow bay and become beached together. Nobody knows why this happens although a few theories have been advanced.

It is possible that the whales may be caught out by the tides or confused by the weather conditions, or they may also be affected by parasites that upset their nervous systems. It has been suggested that they swim into shallow water to scratch themselves on the sandy sea bed, or that shallow water in some way upsets their ability to navigate, perhaps as a result of changes in the earth's magnetic field,

Frequently, a whole herd of pilot whales runs aground together, with most of them pointing in the same direction, along the shore line.

▲ Pilot whales tend to travel in small female-dominated groups of ten or more individuals. They typically travel in a slow, leisurely way, not like the energetic curving surges of dolphins.

▶ The pilot whale's dorsal fin is distinctly hooked – the curvature at the tip is more pronounced in the males.

the Cornish coast. Sometimes other species, particularly dolphins, join the herd for a while. Most herds are formed mainly of females with their partly grown calves and perhaps one or two adult males. The males are said to defend other members of the herd by swimming between the group and potential danger, such as ships.

Pilot whales are equipped with teeth and catch prey, rather than filter plankton

DID YOU KNOW?
There are two species of pilot whale – the long-finned pilot whale found around Britain and a similar, but short-finned, species that lives in the tropics.

as the great baleen whales do. Their upper and lower jaws each carry 16–24 small teeth less than 13mm (⅜in) in diameter. These are simple pegs, used for seizing the prey before it is swallowed. Pilot whales eat squid and cuttlefish mainly, and sometimes fish. As they get older, yearly variations in growth cause rings to develop in the growing teeth. Like the annual rings in a tree trunk, which are also caused by seasonal cycles of growth, these lines can be counted to provide an estimate of a whale's age. Male pilot whales can live to be at least 20 years old and females live longer still. A few individuals may survive for more than 60 years.

The smooth, generally black pilot whale is often called a 'blackfish', although this is misleading because it is a mammal and not a fish, nor is it always black. Older individuals have a pale grey saddle around and behind the dorsal fin and a grey patch under the chin. The belly becomes grey, too, but the extent of this may vary between individuals.

The skin looks very smooth, yet close inspection reveals curious circular pockmarks, especially around the heads of older animals. These are caused by the horny rings found inside the suckers of squids. While grappling with a whale that is trying to eat it, the squid's tentacles wrap around the whale's head and leave these distinctive marks.

Breeding habits
Female pilot whales reach sexual maturity at about six years when they are 3m (10ft) long; males are a little larger and are probably in the region of 12 years old by

the time they are ready to breed. Breeding seems to continue throughout the year, with calves being born at different times in various parts of the North Atlantic.

Pregnancy lasts 14½–15½ months and the newborn calf weighs in at around 70kg (155lb) and measures about 1.75m (5ft 9in) in length. The mother provides milk for her offspring for nearly two years. Rearing a baby pilot whale takes so long that the females do not produce more young for at least three years.

Threats to survival

Modern commercial fishing and pollution both pose threats to pilot whales. Since whales need to breathe air regularly, if they get tangled up in fishermen's nets while they are diving underwater, they inevitably drown. Like many marine creatures, pilot whales may also be adversely affected by industrial chemicals carried down to the sea by rivers. Some whale blubber has been found to contain high levels of poisonous mercury and PCBs (polychlorinated biphenyls) used in the chemical and engineering industries, which may reduce the whale's fertility and thereby threaten future numbers of this mammal.

On the positive side, pilot whales feed mainly on squid, and as a consequence they have probably been less directly affected by the decline in fish populations than some other smaller species of fish-eating whales, such as the common and bottle-nosed dolphins.

▲ It is thought that the pilot whale was given its name by fishermen who observed that a herd seemed to have a clear leader, its pilot. An alternative explanation is that the whales guided fishermen to shoals of fish.

▼ The long, flat back of the pilot whale is a feature that helps in their identification. Pilot whales rarely leap out of the water in the way that dolphins do, although sometimes they raise their heads to have a look around.

WILDLIFE WATCH

Where can I see pilot whales?

● Whale-watching in Britain always involves a good deal of luck. If you keep an eye out when you are walking on headlands in Scotland and western Ireland, you stand a good chance of seeing a fin or two.

● If you ever discover a stranded whale, alive or dead, you should contact the RSPCA or the local coastguard as soon as possible.

● To find out more about whales and dolphins around Britain, contact the Whale and Dolphin Conservation Society on 01225 334511 or visit their website at www.wdcs.org

Recognising terns

As they wheel and swoop through the air, terns often attract attention from afar with their loud, raucous calls. These migratory birds may be observed throughout the summer months before they take flight for winter quarters.

To the uninitiated, terns bear a passing resemblance to gulls. Certainly most species have gull-like plumage patterns, with grey upperparts and white underparts, but there the similarity ends. Rather than adopting an omnivorous or scavenging lifestyle, most terns are specialist feeders whose skilled aerobatics and ability to dive into water enable them to catch live prey, especially small fish.

You only have to watch a group of terns for a short time to appreciate just how powerful they are in flight. It is hardly surprising that the six species seen regularly in British waters – common, Arctic, roseate, Sandwich, little and black terns – are strongly migratory. All but the black tern breed here, arriving in spring and raising their young over the course of summer. After breeding they fly south, with all but one species overwintering mainly off the coasts of Africa.

Intrepid traveller

The exception is the Arctic tern, the world champion of migratory birds. Many individuals spend time in the hostile latitudes of both the Arctic and Antarctic, breeding as far north as the northernmost Arctic, then flying south to take advantage of summer in the southern hemisphere. Those that breed in Britain are at the southern limit of the species' range.

Some Arctic terns are reckoned to cover up to 25,000 miles each year in their migrations, and this does not take into account any day-to-day travels while staying in summer and winter quarters.

To see terns at their most dramatic, it is best to visit them at one of their breeding colonies. Although many are fenced off to prevent disturbance by dogs and people, some colonies, notably those on islands, are often more accessible.

The best known of these is on the Farne Islands in Northumberland. Under the watchful eye of the National Trust, which owns the site, colonies of Arctic terns in particular have thrived. Here birds are able to nest unmolested within inches of paths trodden daily by hundreds of people. Informed visitors to the islands never

Forced into the shallows by changes in the tide, shoaling whitebait have induced a feeding frenzy among these common terns.

arrive without a hat because the terns are renowned for dive-bombing intruders: they will stab with their sharp bills and may even draw blood.

The five British breeding species all nest on the ground in colonies. Despite the fact that there is a degree of protection afforded by nesting at high densities, the birds are vulnerable to ground predators and so islands and remote shingle headlands are generally favoured. The remaining species, the black tern, is essentially a spring and autumn migrant, although isolated pairs have nested here rarely in the past.

EASY GUIDE TO SPOTTING TERNS

Arctic tern

Black tern

Common tern

Sandwich tern

Little tern

Roseate tern

WHAT ARE TERNS?

● All British terns are migratory and can be observed mainly from April to September, but not at all during the winter months.

● Terns belong to a family of birds called the Sternidae. This group belongs to an order called the Charadriiformes along with gulls and waders. Sometimes referred to as 'sea terns' because they live mainly along the coast and hunt in inshore waters, the genus

Sterna includes the common, Arctic, roseate, Sandwich and little terns. The black tern belongs to the genus *Chlidonias* and, along with other members of the genus, is sometimes called a 'marsh tern'.

● Black terns occur mainly on freshwater and coastal marshes. Common terns occur mainly on the coast, but are also seen far inland. The other four species of tern are essentially coastal.

HOW CAN I IDENTIFY TERNS?

● Members of the genus *Sterna* have grey upperparts and white underparts. In most species the cap is black. Black terns have almost entirely black plumage during the breeding season. At other times, it is grey, black and white, the precise pattern depending on the season and the age of the bird.

● Terns have bills that are narrow and sharply pointed. Look at the colour to help identify different species. Common terns have mainly orange-red bills, usually with a black tip; Arctic terns have dark red bills, usually without a black tip; roseate terns have mainly black bills with a red base when breeding (all-dark in spring); little terns have black-tipped yellow bills, while those of black terns are all-dark.

● All terns have relatively long, narrow wings and a distinctly buoyant flight.

● Most species of tern have tails that are forked, although this feature is not always apparent. The length of the tail and degree of forking varies from the short, shallowly forked tail of the black tern to the long, deeply forked tails of the Arctic and roseate terns.

● The Sandwich tern is almost as big as a black-headed gull, while the little tern is smallest of all the tern species. The black tern is only slightly larger than the little tern and can also be distinguished by its dashing, direct flight style.

WILDLIFE WATCH

Where can I see terns?

● To see terns migrating, visit the south coast of Britain in April. Mixed flocks will be moving along the shores at this time.

● Observe little terns at their breeding colonies on south coast estuaries. Since all these sites are protected, you will have to watch the birds from a distance. Sit quietly beside a brackish pool, however, and you may be rewarded with a sighting. The harbours at Rye and Pagham in Sussex, are both good spots.

● For common terns, visit one of the colonies along the north Norfolk coast.

Blakeney Point is one location. Several other tern species breed here as well.

● The Farne Islands are worth visiting to observe Arctic terns. Small numbers of roseate and common terns can also be seen here. The largest colonies of roseates occur on Rockabill Island, off the east coast of Ireland, near Dublin.

● The black tern is an unpredictable species. In some years, many adults pass through in spring, stopping off at gravel pits and lakes in England. In autumn too, juveniles may be seen regularly.

The downy chick of the Arctic tern has the same mottled camouflage colouring as the egg it hatched from. At the first sign of danger, it will crouch motionless.

Distribution map key

■ Present all year round

■ Present during summer months

■ Present during winter months

□ Not present

COMMON TERN *Sterna hirundo*

This medium-sized tern has mostly white plumage, except for grey back and flight feathers and a black cap. The bill is red with a black tip, while the legs and feet are red. When in flight, a pale translucent patch on the flight feathers is visible. Juveniles resemble adults in autumn, but have a ginger-buff wash and pale central panels on the wings.

● SIZE
Length 31–35cm (12½–14in)

● NEST
Shallow scrape with sparse lining of shells or vegetation

● BREEDING
1–3 cream to buff eggs with dark blotches laid from May

● FOOD
Mainly small fish, some shrimps and insects

● HABITAT
Sheltered coasts, large lakes in summer

● VOICE
Persistent grating 'kee-yah' and 'kik-kik' calls

● DISTRIBUTION
Common and widespread summer visitor to British and Irish coasts, many island sites and some freshwater lakes inland

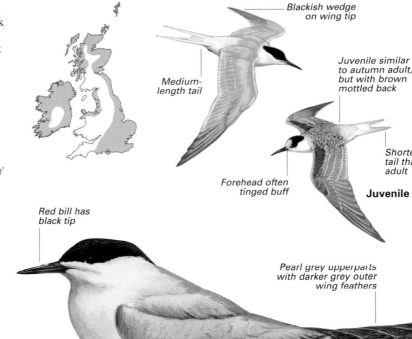

Blackish wedge on wing tip

Medium-length tail

Juvenile similar to autumn adult, but with brown mottled back

Forehead often tinged buff

Shorter tail than adult

Juvenile

Red bill has black tip

Pearl grey upperparts with darker grey outer wing feathers

Medium-length red legs and feet

A black-tipped, orange-red bill is characteristic of the common tern. Its legs, which are also vivid red, are proportionately longer than those of the similar Arctic tern.

ARCTIC TERN *Sterna paradisaea*

Similar to the common tern, the Arctic tern has a shorter, all-red bill, rounder head and shorter legs. Its upperparts are generally paler than the common tern's, while its underparts are greyer and its rump and tail are very white. When viewed from below, all the flight feathers look almost transparent. Juveniles have a white forehead, black cap and grey back; they lack the buff tints of other juvenile terns.

● SIZE
Length 32–35cm (12¾–14in)

● NEST
Shallow scrape on open ground

● BREEDING
1–3 cream to buff eggs with dark blotches laid from May

● FOOD
Mainly small fish, also shrimps and insects

● HABITAT
Rocky coasts and islands; also breeds on some river islands and Scottish isles

● VOICE
Harsh 'kee-aar' and 'kik-kik' calls, slightly higher pitched than common tern's

● DISTRIBUTION
A common summer visitor to northern Britain and much of Ireland

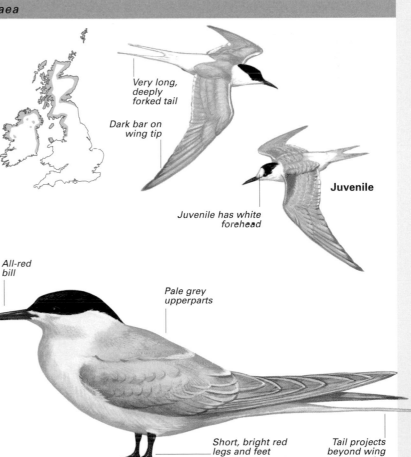

Very long, deeply forked tail

Dark bar on wing tip

Juvenile has white forehead

Juvenile

All-red bill

Pale grey upperparts

Short, bright red legs and feet

Tail projects beyond wing tips

If you catch sight of an Arctic tern standing in its scrape of a nest, you can observe how extremely short its legs are.

ROSEATE TERN *Sterna dougallii*

This medium-sized tern has very long, trailing tail streamers. It has shorter wings than the common tern, and faster, shallower wingbeats. In the breeding season, adults develop a delicate pink flush to the underparts and very pale upperparts. The bill is black with a small patch of red at the base. In winter, the forehead becomes white and the pink flush becomes white. Juveniles have darker blotches on their plumage.

- **SIZE**
Length 33–38cm (13–15in)
- **NEST**
Shallow scrape in sand or shingle
- **BREEDING**
1–2 cream to buff eggs with darker speckles laid April–May
- **FOOD**
Mainly small fish
- **HABITAT**
Exposed coasts with tiny islands
- **VOICE**
Calls include the grating '*kraak*' and the whistling '*chewit*'
- **DISTRIBUTION**
A rare summer visitor to a few coastal sites and offshore islands in Britain and Ireland

Very pale underwings. White forehead and all-black bill. **Juvenile**

Bill is black, often with red base, which becomes more red in late summer

Very pale grey-and-white plumage; much whiter than common or Arctic tern species

Deeply forked tail

Breast flushed pink in spring

Quite long legs and feet, coral red in summer

Seen here in profile, the roseate tern has a slim and elegant outline. It is one of Britain's rarest breeding sea birds.

SANDWICH TERN *Sterna sandvicensis*

This large, pale tern has long, narrow wings and pale grey upperparts with silver-grey flight feathers. In summer, the head is jet black with an untidy crest. The black bill has a yellow tip and the legs and feet are black. From late summer, the forehead becomes white and the black crest is mottled. Juveniles resemble nonbreeding adults but have an all-black bill at first.

- **SIZE**
Length 36–41cm (14¼–16¼in)
- **NEST**
Shallow scrape on shingle or among sand dunes
- **BREEDING**
1–2 whitish or buff blotched eggs laid April–May
- **FOOD**
Mainly small fish
- **HABITAT**
Breeding colonies on sheltered coasts with shallow waters suitable for feeding nearby
- **VOICE**
A harsh, grating '*keerr-ikk*'
- **DISTRIBUTION**
A summer visitor to many parts of coastal Britain and Ireland

Very pale upperparts. Dark cap. **Juvenile**

Jet black cap with shaggy crest

Dark, scaly markings on upperwing and back

Longish black legs and feet

Tail short but deeply forked

The largest of the terns regularly seen in Britain, this species is often the first to arrive, many as early as March. Regularly used colonies are sited on the coast, often on shingle or sand ridges, as well as on islands.

LITTLE TERN *Sterna albifrons*

Only about half the size of a common or Arctic tern, the little tern's narrow wings beat very fast as it hurtles around. Unlike other terns, it has a white forehead in summer as well as in winter. Its yellow bill has a black tip and the legs and feet are orange-yellow. From autumn, there is less black on the head and the bill is all-black. Juveniles have scaly, pale brown on the upperparts, a pale cap and a dark bill.

● SIZE
Length 22–24cm (8½–9½in)

● NEST
Shallow scrape on sand or shingle

● BREEDING
1–3 buff eggs with darker blotches laid April–May

● FOOD
Small fish, also shrimps and insects

● HABITAT
Along coasts, shingle or sand

● VOICE
Rasping, shrill 'keeirr-ink' calls

● DISTRIBUTION
A scarce summer visitor to scattered localities around British and Irish coastlines

Brown-grey markings on back

Flight is hurried, often hovers

Juvenile

Black cap extends through eye

White forehead

Slender yellow bill with black tip

Dark outer flight feathers

The little tern has particularly distinctive head markings and bill colouring. In recent years, many colonies have been lost as a result of disturbance by humans and animal predators.

Orange-yellow legs and feet

BLACK TERN *Chlidonias niger*

A small tern with almost all-dark plumage in summer. Its head and underparts are black, the wings and back a dark, ash-grey. From below, the underwing looks pale grey and the undertail is white. Its bill is black and its legs are dark red. In winter, the upperparts are paler grey, while the underparts become white with a dark patch at the shoulder. Juveniles resemble winter adults. Flight over water is buoyant and erratic.

● SIZE
Length 22–24cm (8½–9½in)

● NEST
Low pile of vegetation close to water

● BREEDING
2–4 cream, spotted eggs laid April–May

● FOOD
Flying insects, aquatic invertebrates and tiny fish

● HABITAT
Freshwater or brackish lakes, reservoirs and marshes, also coasts on migration

● VOICE
Squeaky 'kik-keek' calls

● DISTRIBUTION
A passage migrant through Britain, usually in late summer; has bred here a few times

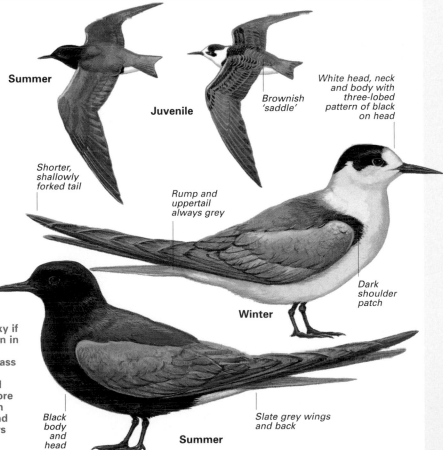

Summer

Juvenile

Brownish 'saddle'

White head, neck and body with three-lobed pattern of black on head

Shorter, shallowly forked tail

Rump and uppertail always grey

Dark shoulder patch

Winter

Count yourself lucky if you see a black tern in breeding plumage, since adults only pass through Britain in small numbers and seldom stay for more than a few hours in any one spot. Inland lakes and reservoirs are favoured sites.

Black body and head

Slate grey wings and back

Summer

The cormorant

Able to dive deeper in search of fish than many other sea birds, the cormorant often strikes a characteristic pose when it emerges from the water.

A cormorant often flies low over water, using slow, powerful wing beats and short glides. Occasionally it soars to great heights, especially when it is travelling over land.

A relative of pelicans and gannets, the cormorant is a large, powerfully built sea bird. On land a cormorant may look awkward and cumbersome, but in flight its long neck and broad wings give it an elegant goose-like appearance. When swimming, the cormorant floats low in the water, like an overloaded boat, with its head held at an angle and tilted slightly upwards.

The cormorant is supremely and notoriously skilful at catching fish. It usually hunts while swimming, with its head and neck dipped under the water, scanning the depths. When a fish is sighted, the bird dives forward, often with a little leap. It pursues nimble prey with ease, using forceful strokes of its feet. All four of the cormorant's toes are webbed

Standing on a rock or breakwater, with wings outstretched to dry in the warm sunshine, the cormorant is a familiar sight all around the coast.

– unlike the duck's toes, only the front three of which are joined. A cormorant regularly dives to 10m (33ft) for 20–30 seconds to catch fish near the sea bed. During a dive, the cormorant's wings are pinned close to its sides.

Swallowing hard

Most of the fish that a cormorant catches measure between 5–15cm (2–6in), although some are much bigger. It eats any small fish it takes immediately, but larger prizes are more difficult to swallow and must be brought to the surface. The cormorant often has to stretch its neck upwards to swallow big fish and may shake its catch around to force it down.

Cormorants are not fussy about the fish they eat. On the coast, they take a lot of flatfish, catching nearly 1kg (up to 2lb) per day. This gets them into trouble with local anglers and fishermen, but only a small proportion of their catch is likely to

WING STRETCH

For many years, the cormorant's typical pose with wings outstretched was believed to be the way that the bird dried its wings. Cormorants have specially modified feather barbs that allow air to escape and water to penetrate the plumage. Although this helps the birds to swim underwater, it soon results in waterlogged plumage. The wing-drying theory seems reasonable, and is still the most likely explanation for this behaviour.

However, another suggestion has been put forward – that the birds are actually warming up their dinner. The fish they catch, especially in deep water, can be very cold and are quite large in relation to the bird's weight – equivalent to a person swallowing whole a 10–20kg (22–44lb) block of ice. Exposing the feathers that cover a stomach full of freezing fish to the warming rays of the sun may ease any discomfort and aid digestion.

CORMORANT FACT FILE

A large aquatic bird, the cormorant is almost prehistoric in appearance. It is found on rocky coasts near shallow bays, mainly in the west of Britain. During the winter, it may also be seen inland around bodies of freshwater, where it often roosts in large numbers in trees.

● NAMES
Common name: cormorant
Scientific name: *Phalacrocorax carbo* (two races in Britain – *P. c. carbo* and *P. c. sinensis*)

● HABITAT
Apart from cliff colonies, a wide range of coastal and inland waters containing fish

● DISTRIBUTION
Throughout Britain in traditional colonies around coast; *sinensis* only from Isle of Wight to Bempton Cliffs on Yorkshire coast

● STATUS
About 12,000 breeding pairs

● SIZE
Length 77–94cm (2ft 6in–3ft 1in); wingspan 1.2–1.5m (4–5ft); weight 2–2.5kg (4½–5½lb)

● KEY FEATURES
Large, heavy, hook-billed sea bird; plumage mainly dark at all ages; breeding birds have white thigh patch and white on face; variable white spray of feathers on crown and nape of neck, especially in winter

● HABITS
Hunts by diving from surface; often seen perched near water, with wings spread, in heraldic pose

● VOICE
Complex and varied when nesting, including deep, guttural growling and cackling calls; otherwise usually silent

● FOOD
Flatfish in sea; eels, roach, trout and perch in freshwater; eats one-fifth of its body weight daily

● BREEDING
Birds return to colonies in early spring; eggs laid late March–June; incubation about 29 days, by both parents; young present in colony from April–September

● NEST
P. c. carbo: large, untidy heap of twigs, seaweed and sometimes other material; built on sheltered cliff ledges, usually less than 100m (110yd) above sea surface, in sea caves or among boulders; *P.c sinensis*: inland in trees

● EGGS
A clutch of 3–4, large, pale blue eggs overlaid with chalky white deposit; incubated for 4 weeks, less in *sinensis*; 1 brood per year

● YOUNG
Fly at 7 weeks; looked after for several more weeks; juveniles brownish with pale underparts.

The hooked bill is large and heavy.

The skin at the base of the bill's under-side is yellow, surrounded by a white area.

The scaly upper wing feathers are bronze.

The bird has a prominent chest.

The plumage is mainly black with bluish and green gloss.

Distribution map key

■	Present all year round
■	Present during winter months
□	Not present

DID YOU KNOW?

In the 17th century, the Stuart kings exploited the cormorant's skill at fishing in much the same way as Chinese fishermen do today.
In China, a cormorant is tethered to a boat by a strong, thin line tied around its neck, which is just tight enough to prevent the bird swallowing the fish it catches and causes the cormorant to brings its prey back to the boat.
In return, the neck cord is released every fifth or sixth fish, allowing the bird to eat its catch as a reward.

The tail is long and strongly wedge shaped.

▲ The mainland European subspecies of cormorant, *P. c. sinensis,* is distinguished by its slimmer build and generally whiter feathering on its neck and head. In Britain, it nests inland in colonies in trees near freshwater lakes and reservoirs.

▶ Young cormorants are cared for by both parents during their 50 days in the nest. When an adult returns from a fishing trip, a chick sticks its head down its parent's throat to make it regurgitate some fish.

be of immediate commercial interest or to damage stocks in the long term.

Cormorants are more of a problem in the winter when they fly inland and treat fish farms and well-stocked, shallow fishing lakes as handy fast-food outlets. These lakes are stocked with large numbers of fish that are just the right size for both cormorants and anglers. A flock of cormorants can have a serious impact on fish stocks and prompt fish farmers to demand a cull or the right to shoot on sight. Some fisheries cover their smaller pools with nets or manage to scare the cormorants away, but at others

cormorants are a growing pest. One long-term solution might be to develop the impoverished underwater habitat of the lakes to give the fish somewhere to hide from the birds. In some farmed lakes, cormorants benefit the salmon stocks by hunting the fish that eat young salmon.

Cormorant versus salmon

On northern rivers, where salmon and trout fishing is a valuable tourist attraction, the situation is different. Here, there is a long-running natural battle

between cormorants and salmon. Since salmon spawn up river and are migratory, the young fish have to run the gauntlet of cormorants waiting at wide and slow-moving stretches on their way down river to the sea. The cormorants' impact has probably been felt more in recent years because young salmon are suffering for other reasons, such as river pollution. However, a decline in the numbers of returning adult salmon – the ones that anglers prize – is unlikely to be due mainly to earlier cormorant predation.

Coming in to land

Most cormorants nest on cliff ledges next to the sea. Some colonies are so densely packed that the nests are actually touching. Negotiating a landing in such crowded conditions is tricky for these bulky birds.

With its legs held well back, the cormorant's neck and body are almost vertical as it 'stalls' and comes to a virtual stop in midair.

As a cormorant approaches its cliff-ledge nest, its slimline body and webbed feet are clearly visible.

CORMORANT CALENDAR

JANUARY • FEBRUARY

Throughout the winter, cormorants may be seen inland on freshwaters, as well as all coasts. In very cold weather, the inland birds retreat to unfrozen brackish waters in estuaries.

MARCH • APRIL

In March, the native cormorants return to their cliff-ledge breeding sites to lay a single clutch of three or four eggs. The eggs are incubated by both the male and the female.

MAY • JUNE

Image shown.

The young hatch and, on average, remain in the nest for just under two months. Their parents will travel long distances to find fish for their hungry offspring.

JULY • AUGUST

The first young birds fledge, but they often stay around the colony for some time, hoping to be fed by their parents. Gradually, the bonds between adults and young break down.

SEPTEMBER • OCTOBER

The birds begin to disperse from coastal colonies. Some move inland, while others fly south to the Continent. At this time of year, cormorants may be seen almost anywhere.

NOVEMBER • DECEMBER

Coastal cormorants now move to inland waters to overwinter, returning to the same areas each year. Numbers of *P. c. sinensis* are boosted by a small influx of birds from Europe.

To slow itself down, the cormorant fans its tail to increase wind resistance and act as a brake.

A few powerful wing beats control the descent as the head and feet move forwards for touch down.

The returning bird is usually greeted by its mate with a pointing display. The bird points its head and neck diagonally upwards, swaying as it does so.

THE SHAG

Britain's only other native cormorant is the shag. *Phalacrocorax aristotelis*, a widespread breeder. An elegant sea bird, the adult shag has a distinctive, metallic green sheen to its plumage – especially during the breeding season – which becomes duller in winter. This colouring gave rise to an old name for the shag, the green cormorant.

The shag has bright green eyes and a slender bill with a yellow base. Early in the breeding season, it also has a short crest on the forehead, but this is lost by midsummer.

Shags are essentially coastal birds and are rarely found in freshwater habitats. Following severe gales or foggy spells on the coast, they may occasionally turn up on inland waters; after very bad weather, small flocks are sometimes found on large gravel pits or reservoirs in southern England. Most recorded inland sightings, however, refer to individual birds – often juveniles from the previous summer's broods. As with other sea birds, these records of vagrant birds are known as 'wrecks'. They most frequently occur in autumn and early winter when the weather is bad, but their occurrence is unpredictable and does not necessarily happen every year.

Shags are found in loose colonies at the base of cliffs all around the rocky coasts of Britain and Ireland. Their numbers have increased in recent years and in some places continue to do so. They are now more common than cormorants, outnumbering them by almost four to one.

Although similar in appearance to cormorants, the two species do not compete for food. The shag takes mainly free-swimming fish from mid-water and generally hunts in

Smaller and slimmer than the cormorant, the shag is distinguished by its finer bill, thinner neck, iridescent green plumage and, early in the breeding season, a jaunty, upstanding crest.

Shag chicks remain in the nest for seven or eight weeks. The adults are vigorous in the defence of their brood and thrust their beaks menacingly at intruders.

deeper water. Typical prey species are smaller than those taken by cormorants, and include sand eels and members of the herring and cod families.

Most breeding shags start building nests in January and February and lay a clutch of three or four eggs in late March or April. Both parents share the incubation: from egg-laying to fledging takes 12 to 13 weeks. The parents continue to care for their chicks for a few weeks after fledging.

Nesting colonies

Most traditional colonies of cormorants are found on low, rocky coastal islets. Once the male has claimed a ledge, he advertises for a mate by sitting on his nest site and looking upwards, then raising his wings up and outwards, then closing them again. It seems that female cormorants find flashes of the breeding male's white thigh patches appealing.

◄ An eel is a slippery catch, but with the cormorant's strong, hooked bill clamped around its writhing body, it is unlikely to escape. The cormorant may toss the eel into the air before swallowing it.

Nesting cormorants indulge in complex displays, which contrast to the way in which they ignore each other while fishing. On leaving or returning to the nest site, a pair of cormorants display to each other by opening the bill, snaking their necks and making guttural calls. The male is particularly flamboyant, raising his tail and flinging his head back to touch its base with his closed beak. At the same time, he swings his head from side to side and makes gargling sounds.

It is very important that one member of the pair stays at the nest at all times. Nesting sites on a cliff face are at such a premium that even an empty nest is a valuable resource; the nesting material might be stolen by other cormorants building nearby – or worse, an interloper may claim the site.

The nest is an untidy heap of seaweed and branches lined with some finer material. Here, three or four chalky blue eggs are incubated for about a month. The hatchlings are naked at first with blackish brown skin; thick dark brown down grows after about one week.

◄ Cormorants often roost in groups, and a particularly good perch is guarded jealously. The adult bird with its head thrown back is making it clear that it is not going to vacate its perch for the juvenile with the pale breast, even if it is one of its own offspring.

A roosting cormorant inflates the loose pouch of bare yellow skin on its throat – the gular pouch – before launching itself into the air. This display communicates that it is about to take flight.

On hot days, the young birds pant with their throats distended. Fluttering the loose skin of the throat pouch is a special form of panting that enables the birds to cool down rapidly. The quick breaths and palpitation of the throat enable the bird to lose body heat to the air flow and thus cool down.

On the increase

Over the last 30 or 40 years, cormorants have become an increasingly familiar sight on inland freshwater lakes, reservoirs and larger rivers during the autumn and winter. In the last 15 years, cormorants have even started to breed on inland waters, particularly in the south-east of England. DNA analysis shows that these inland nesting birds are genetically distinct from native cormorants: they belong to a European subspecies known as *Phalacrocorax carbo sinensis*. Individuals are slightly smaller with more white in their breeding plumage. Native cormorants breed on sea cliffs and rarely gather in colonies bigger than 200 pairs. *Sinensis*, however, frequently forms large colonies inland – some with more than 1000 pairs. Trees with several cormorant nests are often killed by the accumulation of bird droppings known as guano.

Cormorants do not undertake defined migrations, but a small proportion of British birds disperses across several hundred miles after breeding. They cross the English Channel to France and even reach north-west Spain.

For a cormorant, the most arduous part of fishing is taking off from the water. Its weight increased by waterlogged feathers and a load of fish, the bird has to expend considerable energy to become airborne.

WILDLIFE WATCH

Where can I see cormorants and shags?

● In Britain and Ireland, almost any large stretch of water – salt, fresh or brackish – that has a good population of fish is likely to support cormorants at some stage during the year.

● The most interesting place to watch cormorants is at their roosts. These are often in trees – preferably on islands – or on structures jutting out from the water, such as abstraction towers, jetties (particularly old, ruined ones) or simply lines of posts. In some areas, where roosting sites are at a premium, overhead wires and pylons are also used; on extremely big ones coming from power stations, perches may be 80–100m (260–330ft) high. Roosts are communal and are either used in the day or both day and night. Large numbers of birds from a wide area gather at night-time roosts. Good feeding sites may be as far as 48km (30 miles) away.

● Most traditional sea-cliff colonies are remote, and the cormorants can be very flighty. They may be visible with a telescope, but are rarely easy to watch. The new colonies that include *P. c. sinensis* in trees are often easier to see. Two good sites are the huge colony at Abberton Reservoir in Essex, where about 500 pairs can generally be seen breeding, and a smaller colony at Little Paxton, near St Ives in Cambridgeshire. There are other colonies in the London area, especially at Walthamstow Reservoirs, and also near Nottingham and at Rutland Water.

● Shags are likely to be seen on the sea or near the cliffs of rocky shores and headlands, but seldom inland. The birds often form small flocks on low rocks, where they stand erect, their thinner bills and necks and steeper foreheads distinguishing them from cormorants.

Recognising crabs

Sharp eyes are needed to spot crabs, since they seek shelter from their predators and the elements wherever possible on the seashore. Clues to their types lie in the shape and colour of their shells.

Crabs are Britain's most familiar seashore inhabitants. These crustaceans play a vital part in the ecology of the seashore, acting both as scavengers and predators, as well as being a source of food for other creatures, including some fish and sea birds. Roughly 50 species of crab inhabit the shores of the British Isles, but only about ten of these are at all widespread. The common shore crab is the most abundant, and – with its dark green or red shell – the easiest to recognise.

Crab anatomy
Crabs have five pairs of legs. Of these, the first pair takes the form of claws, or pincers, while the rest are modified for walking or swimming. The claws are often very powerful and are used for defence, fighting for mates and obtaining food. Females have smaller claws than males.

The body of the crab is protected by a flat shell, or carapace, the shape and colour of which is usually the most easily identifiable feature of each species. The segmented abdomen, or 'tail', of the crab is small and permanently folded beneath the shell. The female may carry her mass of eggs beneath the flap.

The eyes of the crab are stalked and lie on either side of one or more pairs of antennae. Below these are 'mouthparts', which are used for feeding.

Crustaceans have to moult in order to grow, so periodically the crab sheds its old shell and the soft skin beneath expands and then hardens. After about ten such moults, the crab reaches its full size and thereafter moults only once a year. Crabs are

Spider crabs are named for their long, spindly legs and the strong spines or 'tubercules' on their shells. When stranded by the tide, these large crabs usually wedge their squat bodies among rocks, camouflaging themselves with seaweed and other debris.

vulnerable while moulting and go into hiding until their new shells have toughened.

The female often lays a huge number of eggs, on average around 150,000. The eggs hatch into minute larvae that disperse into the sea. Those larvae that survive metamorphose, or undergo a change in form and structure, into miniature adults. These eventually descend to the sea bed and begin the process of moulting and growing. Some, such as the edible crab, may survive for up to 20 years.

One group of crabs, the hermit crabs, are unusual in that they alone lack a true shell, relying instead on the abandoned shells of molluscs for protection. A hermit crab has claws and legs like other crabs, but its curious worm-like body is soft, reduced and twisted. In order to grow, it first sheds the shell-like covering on its claws and front legs. Then, after a careful inspection of empty shells in the vicinity, it simply takes possession of a new, larger one.

WILDLIFE WATCH

Where can I see crabs?

● Summer is the best time to look for most crab species. Rocky shores usually offer the best opportunities for discovery.

● Lift clumps of seaweed or turn over rocks at low tide, and you may discover crabs hiding underneath. Always remember to replace the seaweed and turn back the rocks so that the crustaceans can continue with their lives. Most crabs will not survive long out of water on hot days, so be sure to return them to the rock pool or the sea after a few minutes.

EASY GUIDE TO SPOTTING CRABS

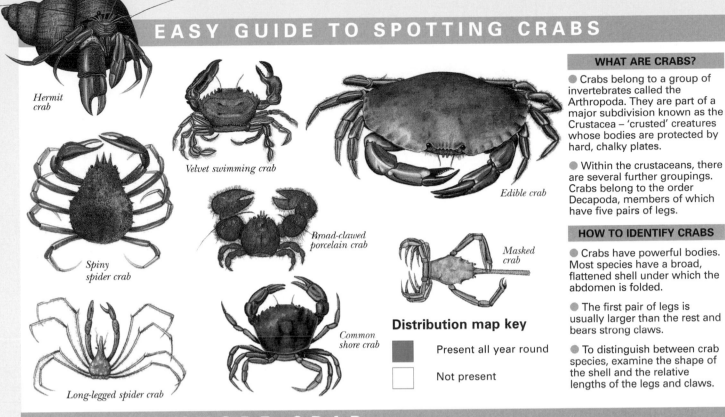

Hermit crab

Velvet swimming crab

Edible crab

Spiny spider crab

Broad-clawed porcelain crab

Masked crab

Long-legged spider crab

Common shore crab

WHAT ARE CRABS?

● Crabs belong to a group of invertebrates called the Arthropoda. They are part of a major subdivision known as the Crustacea – 'crusted' creatures whose bodies are protected by hard, chalky plates.

● Within the crustaceans, there are several further groupings. Crabs belong to the order Decapoda, members of which have five pairs of legs.

HOW TO IDENTIFY CRABS

● Crabs have powerful bodies. Most species have a broad, flattened shell under which the abdomen is folded.

● The first pair of legs is usually larger than the rest and bears strong claws.

● To distinguish between crab species, examine the shape of the shell and the relative lengths of the legs and claws.

Distribution map key

■ Present all year round

□ Not present

COMMON SHORE CRAB *Carcinus maenas*

Also known as the green shore crab, this species can be very aggressive if it is handled. The edge of its shell has three lobes between the eyes and five sharp points on either side of each eye. In summer, the female often carries a mass of orange eggs under her tail.

If threatened, the common shore crab spreads its claws.

● SIZE
Shell diameter up to 6cm (2½in)

● COLOUR
Usually green with variable patterning; older adults black above and orange underneath

● DISTRIBUTION
Widespread

● HABITAT
Common on most seashores, including estuaries and salt marshes, even where water is brackish or slightly polluted

VELVET SWIMMING CRAB *Necora puber*

Distinguished by its flattened shell, which is covered with a dense velvety covering of dark, muddy brown hairs, this crab also has bristly, paddle-like legs to help propel it through the water. It is extremely aggressive and powerful.

The joints of the legs are usually conspicuously marked with red and blue.

● SIZE
Shell diameter up to 6.5cm (2½in)

● COLOUR
Dull brown with patches of red on insides of claws, displayed when crab is disturbed; eyes also red

● DISTRIBUTION
Common and widespread

● HABITAT
Rocky shores, from lower shore down to deeper water

EDIBLE CRAB *Cancer pagurus*

The edible crab is easily recognised by the 'pie-crust' edge to its shell and its colour. The largest of the common crab species in Britain, it can weigh up to several pounds. This crab feeds mainly on other shellfish.

The edible crab's black-tipped claws are massive, especially in the male, and very powerful.

● SIZE
Shell length up to 14cm (5½in), width over 25cm (10in)

● COLOUR
Reddish orange or pinkish brown, underside dirty cream

● DISTRIBUTION
Widespread

● HABITAT
Common on wide range of sheltered, rocky shores

SPINY SPIDER CRAB *Maja squinado*

Also known as the common or thornback spider crab, it has a large, oval shell which usually has a prickly or spiny texture. In addition, spindly, hairy legs and long, slender claws give a spider-like look.

This spider crab is often found lurking in rock pools. Its spiny shell, can be painful if accidentally trodden upon.

- **SIZE**
  Shell length up to 20cm (8in), claws up to 45cm (17¾in)
- **COLOUR**
  Orange when clean, often covered with algae and encrusting animals
- **DISTRIBUTION**
  Common off southern and south-western coasts
- **HABITAT**
  On or near low watermark on rocks and coarse sand

LONG-LEGGED SPIDER CRAB *Macropodia rostrata*

This small species has a triangular-shaped shell, short claws, long, thin legs and prominent eyes. There are many similar species of spider crab, all of which are expertly camouflaged.

Spider crabs are adept at concealing themselves with algae, sponges and other marine debris.

- **SIZE**
  Shell length up to 2.2cm (¾in), claws up to 2.5cm (1in)
- **COLOUR**
  Greyish to yellowish or reddish brown
- **DISTRIBUTION**
  Common on sheltered rocky shores, mainly in the south
- **HABITAT**
  Weed-infested pools and gullies near the low watermark

MASKED CRAB *Corystes cassivelaunus*

Furrows on this crab's oval shell resemble a human face, hence its common name. Two distinctive, long, bristly antennae protrude from between the eyes, forming a breathing tube when the crab is buried.

On wet sand the masked crab quickly burrows out of sight, disappearing tail-first at surprising speed.

- **SIZE**
  Shell length up to 4cm (1½in)
- **COLOUR**
  Light brown with flesh tones on the shell and legs
- **DISTRIBUTION**
  Widespread, but most common in the south
- **HABITAT**
  Normally remains buried in clean sand, at or below the low watermark

HERMIT CRAB *Pagurus bernhardus*

The hermit crab lacks a hard shell to protect itself and takes refuge by coiling its body inside a discarded shell, often one from a sea snail, such as a whelk. It has large, rough claws of uneven size and eyes on long stalks.

A sea anemone may live on the borrowed shell. Its stinging tentacles help to protect the hermit crab from enemies.

- **SIZE**
  Length, including claws, up to 10cm (4in)
- **SHELL**
  Mollusc shell, sometimes covered with algae and encrusting animals
- **DISTRIBUTION**
  Found around all coasts, but most common in the south
- **HABITAT**
  Pools and gullies on the middle to lower shore; larger specimens in deeper water

BROAD-CLAWED PORCELAIN CRAB *Porcellana platycheles*

Its claws are flattened and densely haired, as are the legs and shell. A similar long-clawed porcelain crab (*P. longicornis*) has a slightly smaller, smooth shell and long, slender claws.

Spines on the end of its walking legs help to anchor the porcelain crab to rocks.

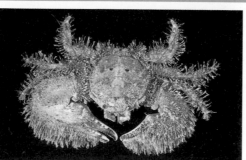

- **SIZE**
  Shell diameter up to 1.5cm (⅝in)
- **COLOUR**
  Underside creamy white with a sheen, giving rise to common name
- **DISTRIBUTION**
  Common around most of coastline, especially in the south
- **HABITAT**
  Under boulders and in silt-filled crevices on sheltered, rocky shores

The starfish

Starfish may appear to be merely decorative rock-pool ornaments, but in fact these colourful seashore residents have formidable strength and a voracious appetite.

The burrowing starfish has an unusually smooth surface, which enables it to slip away under the sand.

The starfish has evolved some quite extraordinary characteristics. It has five arms but no head, it can change direction without turning round, it pushes its stomach outside its body to feed, and it can regrow a missing limb. It has a highly original way of moving, too, using water pressure to operate a system of tube-feet.

These amazing creatures belong to an extremely successful and diverse group of animals called echinoderms, which also includes sea urchins, sea cucumbers, brittlestars and featherstars. Since first appearing more than 550 million years ago, starfish have dispersed throughout the oceans, from the fringes of the sea down to its greatest depths, and have become dominant members of the sea-bed community.

Spiny skin

The name 'echinoderm' comes from the Greek for 'spiny skin', and the surface of the starfish is covered with many small spines. They grow from the skeleton, which is made up of hard, spiky, crystallised chalk plates called ossicles. Each starfish has a patchwork of these armoured plates laced together with ligaments to form a rigid but flexible frame, which can bend with the animal and protect its internal structures from the assaults and pressures of the sea.

The spines discourage predators from attacking. Those on the upper surface are modified to act together in pairs like little tweezers. They keep the outer surface clear of unwelcome colonisers by pinching and squashing the larvae of any sedentary animal that may attempt to settle on the starfish and use it as a mobile base.

The skin covering the body, including the spines, secretes a distasteful mucus that also helps to keep every part of the surface clean. Any particle of food settling on the top is detected by touch sensitive sense cells and carried on a conveyor belt of mucus towards the mouth. If the starfish is left high and dry by a falling tide, the mucus covering its body keeps it moist enough to survive for a short while.

Dealing with pressure

From above and below, the starfish looks symmetrical, with five tapering arms radiating out from a central disc. The mouth is located in the centre of the underside of the disc. There is one structure that breaks the otherwise radial symmetry of the body. On the central disc, slightly off-centre between the origins of two adjacent arms, is a small flat plate called the madreporite. This plate is pierced by hundreds of tiny canals, and its principal function is to equalise pressure between the hydraulic system in the

The tips of the starfish's arms are equipped with sensitive tube-feet, allowing it to feel where it is going and to investigate around corners.

DID YOU KNOW?

The group name for starfish is *Asteroida,* from the Greek for star. The common starfish is *Asterias rubens,* meaning 'red star'.

TUBE-FEET

Starfish move using a system of interconnected, hydraulically operated tube-feet that project from the body in two rows down each arm. Each one is connected to a bag-like reservoir, called the ampulla, which contracts to force water into the tube-foot so that it extends. Muscles in each tube-foot can bend it in any direction. While the starfish is moving, half the tube-feet are being extended and the other half are contracting. The combined action of all the tube-feet moves the starfish slowly over the sea bed.

In the common starfish, most of the tube-feet are used for walking, so the ends are equipped with suckers that temporarily stick to the rock. The attachment/detachment cycle is actually more complex than the structure of the sucker suggests. When attached to a windscreen or a tiled wall, a rubber sucker takes some shifting and may even need a thumbnail pushed under its edge to break the seal, yet the starfish manages to detach each tube-foot quite easily.

The reason lies in the mucus produced by the starfish. Each sucker has mucous glands. These secrete droplets of a sticky substance that helps the sucker to adhere to the rock surface. When the sucker is to be detached, another set of mucous

If you hold a starfish upside-down underwater you can see how its tube-feet wave around, seeking a solid surface for their suckers to grip.

glands is activated, this time exuding a very watery secretion that immediately dilutes the sticky mucus, so the sucker on that foot now offers little resistance to the pull of the tube-foot retractor muscles.

The tube-feet have another function, too. The starfish uses those at the ends of the arms to 'smell' the presence of food, and then brings the other tube-feet into play to capture and overpower the prey.

◄ Each tube-foot can be independently extended to various lengths. The suckers at the ends of the tube-feet hold onto the rock over which the animal is moving.

arm assumes dominance at some time, then another arm takes the lead, but there seems to be no particular order in the selection.

There are other fascinating features of starfish locomotion. While the tube-feet of the leading arm swing forwards and back in the direction that the arm is heading, those of the other four arms have to swing sideways at an angle, depending on which way the arm is aligned. How this complex ability is organised with the starfish's minimal nervous system remains a mystery.

Sense of direction

If a starfish is lifted from the surface of the coral reef and immediately replaced on the same spot, it always starts moving uphill. Such a response to disturbance is generally advantageous, because when a starfish loses its footing it often ends up falling to a deeper level. Automatically heading uphill should eventually bring it back to its original level in shallower waters, where the feeding opportunities are often richer than at greater depths.

▼ Starfish populations appear to fluctuate hugely. In some years they occur in such abundance that they threaten other wildlife; at other times they all but disappear from areas where they were previously prolific.

▶ A tangled mass of starfish like this is usually in the throes of a slow-motion feeding frenzy, at the centre of which is their hapless victim – in this case, a large scallop.

starfish's tube-feet, which it uses to move, and the surrounding sea water. Such a device is necessary so that the starfish can move at any depth – tidal rise and fall exerts varying water pressure on the animal, as does a fall into deeper water from an underwater cliff. The madreporite also provides a topping-up point for the tube-foot system if it loses fluid.

Best arm forward?

As a radially symmetrical animal, a starfish has no front or back end, or even a single leading arm. Having remained in one place for a time, while it is feeding perhaps, a starfish can move off with any one of its arms leading. After a while, it may change direction so that another arm points the way forward.

The movement is coordinated and controlled by groups of nerve cells, called ganglia, arranged along each arm. According to how these interact, one

STARFISH FEEDING

Most starfish are active predators with a rather gruesome way of tackling their prey. The favourite food of the common starfish is the common mussel. The two shells of a bivalve mollusc, such as a mussel, look as though they provide secure protection, but they are no match for a determined starfish. It hugs the two shells in its arms, gets a good grip with the suction cups on the end of its tube-feet and, slowly but surely, pulls on the shells until the muscles holding them together start to tire.

When a crack appears between the mollusc's two shells, the starfish pushes its stomach out through its mouth and into the crack, where it begins to secrete digestive juices directly onto the mollusc's body. The tissues of the mollusc are liquefied by the juices into a seafood soup, which is absorbed by the lining of the stomach. The whole meal may take up to eight hours to complete.

That single meal can last the starfish several weeks, but if food is abundant they take advantage and feed voraciously. Not surprisingly, they are attracted to the oyster and mussel-beds at shell fisheries.

The starfish stomach is incredibly delicate. Inside the body it is tightly folded; it expands only when pushed out of the mouth, exposing a large surface area through which food is absorbed.

The sensitive tube-feet at the tips of the starfish arms are used to 'smell' the water around it. They can detect tiny amounts of the chemicals given off by their favourite prey – shellfish such as mussels and cockles.

Just as the starfish can detect the mussel, the mussel senses the starfish, and quickly clamps its shells together with two powerful muscles.

The starfish straddles the mussel, grips the shell with its tube-feet, then pulls with a force equivalent to as much as 5kg (11lb). Eventually, the mollusc's muscles weaken and its shells gape slightly apart.

Internal arrangements

There is little more to a starfish's innards than a gut and a reproductive system. The mouth is in the centre of the underside, and the vent for excreting waste is positioned dead-centre on the upperside. These two openings are connected by the stomach. In addition, there are double side branches, called caeca, down each arm, into which partly digested food is passed for final breakdown and absorption into storage cells in the wall of the gut. The cells are filled during the early summer, and there the food remains until the start of the reproductive season, when eggs and sperm begin to develop in the ovaries or testes.

This is when the gut comes into its own. The stored food nourishes the maturing sex cells over the winter. By the following spring, the food is at its lowest level of the year and the reproductive tissues are fully developed: the starfish is ready to spawn.

Most starfish reproduce by collectively releasing their eggs or sperm into the water. The sperm fertilise the eggs, which develop into tiny transparent larvae. These spend the next month or so drifting around with a mass of other tiny larvae in the plankton before settling and metamorphosing into tiny starfish.

A few species, including the British cushion star and bloody Henry, do things rather differently. Their young do not go through a separate larval stage but emerge from the eggs as tiny starfish. Instead of abandoning them to the perils of the open ocean, these so-called brooding starfish keep them safely in a place under the mouth between the arms, ceasing their own feeding activities during this caring period so that the babies do not get swallowed by mistake.

▲ Cushion stars are usually quite small. They have short, rounded rays forming a cushion like body. Their upper surface is covered with short, stiff spines.

◄ Spiny starfish vary in colour from grey or greenish to reddish or pinkish. They are mostly found in north and west Britain and Ireland and may grow as large as 80cm (32in) across.

Shoreline homes

The common starfish is the species most likely to be encountered on Britain's shores, particularly washed up on the high-water line or in rock pools. Cushion stars are seen on rocky reefs. On sandy beaches, you occasionally see a sand star that has surfaced for some reason. It usually lies just under the surface of the sand with only the tips of its arms protruding so that it can take food and oxygen from a current of water.

The common starfish, cushion star and sand star all have flattened arms to withstand the pull of the sea on the shore, but the bloody Henry has rounded arms and usually lives just below tide-level. It feeds either by floating in the water with upturned arms, catching particles of food, or by finding encrusting organisms on the rocks and using the usual starfish method of turning the stomach inside-out and digesting its food externally.

Regrowing arms

Before much was known about starfish, fishermen would drag a large mop over the beds to collect them, then tear each one apart and throw the bits back, little realising that starfish have great powers of regeneration. After such treatment, each part could regenerate into a whole animal again, so the fishermen were increasing the menace to their precious shellfish.

If a starfish loses one of its five arms, it can regrow the missing limb. Sometimes you come across starfish with four equal-sized arms and a much smaller one that is in the process of regrowing. In some starfish, as long as there is one arm attached to one-fifth of the central plate, it can completely recover to be a perfect, five-pointed symmetrical star again.

EXCEPTIONS TO THE FIVE-ARM RULE

Of the 17 species of British starfish, three depart from the familiar five-armed symmetry – the seven-armed starfish and the two species of sunstar. All start their juvenile lives with five arms. The seven-armed adds another two, and the sunstars may total up to 13 or 14 arms. The reason that most British species have five arms is probably because, at a critical stage in their development, the skeleton of chalky plates is stronger if it has an odd number in the ring; three would be too few to encircle the internal organs, and seven or more too many.

▲ The raised tips of the common sunstar not only bear the most sensitive tube-feet, but also have a tiny light-sensitive pad – the starfish equivalent of an eye – which draws it towards/away from light.

◄ The seven-armed starfish develops from a microscopic swimming larval stage, which settles on the sea bed and slowly changes into a perfect miniature juvenile.

Rock pools at low tide are the best onshore places to look for starfish. They are not harmful to humans, so by all means pick them up for a closer look, but don't pull them from rocks if they are well attached, and always put them back in the water.

WILDLIFE WATCH

Where can I see starfish?

● Starfish are generally intolerant of long periods of exposure, and the best place to see them behaving naturally is underwater, by snorkelling or scuba diving.

● Look for starfish in the lowest rock pools at low tide – be careful not to get trapped – or wander along the strand line after high tide, especially after rough weather.

● Starfish are displayed in most marine aquaria. Watching one climb the glass is the ideal way to see the coordinated movements of their tube-feet.

● Dried starfish are often sold in seaside shops along with shells and other souvenirs. Stop and think before you buy one as a bathroom ornament. Unlike the shell left behind when a mollusc dies, this was taken out of the sea as a living animal.

Recognising seashells

Searching for shells is one of the most pleasurable of seaside activities, since so many types can be found on the beach. Look for periwinkles and limpets in rocky places or scan sandy shores for cockles and scallops.

The shells you find on the seashore are mostly empty. Each one once housed a marine mollusc, a soft-bodied creature that lives in the wet sand. Burrowing into the sand helps it to avoid predators, while the tide delivers food in the form of seaweed and algae, or other tiny organisms.

When the original inhabitant dies and the mollusc shell is abandoned, it may provide a home for other small creatures, such as crabs and sea anemones, before it is finally ground down by the action of the waves and mixes into the grains of sand on the beach.

Marine molluscs

Molluscs are one of the largest groups in the animal kingdom with more than 100,000 recorded species. Most of them live in the sea, but some have taken to the land (garden snails and slugs), while others have adapted to freshwater (mussels and snails).

The majority of molluscs that live in the sea are either gastropods or bivalves. Gastropods live inside a single shell and can be divided into 'sea snails' and sea slugs. Snail species often have coiled shells and a muscular

This flat periwinkle species, *Littorina mariae*, lives and breeds on toothed wrack seaweed.

foot that helps the mollusc to move. Examples include the painted topshell, the common periwinkle, and the whelk. A typical gastropod's small head usually bears a pair of sensory tentacles that each have a simple eye at the base. Inside its mouth is a rough, ribbon-like structure, called the radula, that rasps food from the rocks and attacks

A sharply pointed conical shape and pink stripes make the painted topshell easy to identify. It is found under stones at low tide.

prey. A single gill aids respiration by taking up oxygen from the water.

Many of the shells found on the beach, however, are bivalves and typical species include the cockle, scallop and pod razor shell. Bivalves have two flattened shells, known as valves, that are held together by a ligament. Two muscles clamp the shell shut, and a muscular foot is used for movement in the water or burrowing in the sand. A pair of internal gills filter oxygen and food, in the form of tiny particles and microscopic organisms, from the water.

WILDLIFE WATCH

Where can I find seashells?

● Almost any stretch of seashore will yield shells, but some places are better than others. Maps and signs offer clues – for example, any place called 'Shell Bay' would be worth exploring.

● An exposed, sandy beach after a storm is usually a good source of shells. The strand line is the best place to look, but remember that shells are positioned by the tides, with the largest shells remaining near the low watermark.

● Search narrow, sandy gullies, as waves tend to concentrate shells in small channels and depressions.

● Never collect live molluscs and always check seemingly empty shells for new residents.

EASY GUIDE TO SPOTTING SEASHELLS

One shell or two?

Seashells come in two basic forms. Gastropod molluscs have a single, asymmetrical shell, but bivalve molluscs have paired shells, or valves, which are usually symmetrical. When a bivalve dies, its two halves often separate and collectors may find only one half on the beach.

Single, spirally coiled shell

Pointed spire

Edible mussel
Mytilus edulis

Two shells joined together by tough elastic ligament

Common whelk
Buccinium undatum

Shell lined with mother-of-pearl

WHAT ARE SEASHELLS?

● Seashells are the hard, chalky cases that protect the soft bodies of many species of marine mollusc. The concentric rings found on all shells indicate the stages of growth.

● The shell is secreted by the outer layers of the mollusc's mantle. The mantle is the soft layer of tissue that protects the part of the mollusc's body that lies inside the shell.

● The shell comprises three layers. The outer layer is called the periostracum and is composed of a protein called conchiolin, which is extracted from the mollusc's food. The middle layer is made up of calcite, a form of calcium carbonate. The inner layer – the nacreous layer – is also composed of calcium carbonate and is laid down in thin layers throughout the mollusc's life. These can give the shell's inner lining a pearly appearance, when it is called mother-of-pearl, or nacre.

Distribution map key

◻ Not present

◼ Present all year round

EDIBLE (OR COMMON) PERIWINKLE *Littorina littorea*

Often collected for food, this abundant species feeds on microscopic algae that coat the rocks. The shell is thick, rounded and coiled, and terminates in a sharp point. It is usually dark brown in colour, with fine lines.

The edible periwinkle's shell varies in colour, but is always rough and sculpted with concentric lines.

● SIZE
Height up to 3cm (1¼in)

● HABITAT
Common from upper to lower zones of rocky shores, often on rocks among dense beds of brown algae; also in muddy estuaries

● DISTRIBUTION
Widespread

FLAT PERIWINKLE *Littorina obtusata*

This periwinkle has a smooth, rounded shell that terminates in a very short, flattened spire. Shells vary in colour from dark brown to almost white, and many are orange or yellow. Empty shells may form deep deposits on beaches near rocky shores.

Thanks to the round shape of its shell, the flat periwinkle resembles a colourful bean or pulse, especially when seen en masse.

● SIZE
Height up to 1cm (½in)

● HABITAT
Very common on mid–low zones of sheltered, rocky shores, usually among brown algae

● DISTRIBUTION
Widespread

PAINTED TOPSHELL *Calliostoma zizyphinum*

With its circular opening and conical, coiled shell – which terminates in a distinct point – the empty painted topshell is frequently adopted by small hermit crabs. Clean specimens usually show a pattern of orange, red and yellow markings.

The colourful painted topshell looks like an old-fashioned spinning top.

● SIZE
Height up to 2.5cm (1in)

● HABITAT
Common on rocks and among kelp found on lower shore

● DISTRIBUTION
Most common on Britain's south-west coast

COMMON LIMPET *Patella vulgata*

The distinctive common limpet has a simple, conical shell that is often covered with encrusting organisms. The inner surface is usually very smooth and shiny. A muscular foot firmly anchors this species to rocks to withstand even the harshest storms.

The outer surface of the shell of the common limpet is greyish white and ridged.

● SIZE
Length up to 6cm (2½in)

● HABITAT
Common on all rocky coasts; sometimes seen in large colonies; shell shape varies according to exposure of site

● DISTRIBUTION
Widespread

DOG WHELK *Nucella lapillus*

Easily recognised by its thick, coiled shell, the dog whelk has a ridged outer surface and a deep groove running along one side of the opening. The shell terminates in a sharp point and is usually whitish in colour, but may be marked by brown bands.

The dog whelk feeds mainly on barnacles and mussels. Its shell is robust and thickly armoured, especially around the lip.

● SIZE
Height up to 4cm (1½in)

● HABITAT
Most common on exposed, rocky shores; often found alongside its eggs, which resemble grains of barley

● DISTRIBUTION
Widespread

COMMON WHELK *Buccinum undatum*

Encrusting tube worms and barnacles often cover the large, coiled shell of the common whelk, which is usually a dirty white colour. Hermit crabs are known to occupy empty shells, as may sea anemones.

Clusters of rounded, papery eggs can often be found on the strand line near the common whelk's heavily ridged shell.

● SIZE
Length up to 10cm (4in)

● HABITAT
Common on muddy and sandy sea beds, mainly just below low-tide level

● DISTRIBUTION
Widespread

PELICAN'S FOOT *Aporrhais pespelicani*

Named after the flared arms of its lip, which form a webbed 'foot' in adults, the pelican's foot shell is undoubtedly striking. It is off-white and pointed, with beaded whorls.

The spiky appearance of the pelican's foot shell is probably an adaptation that protects the mollusc from predation by flatfish.

● SIZE
Length up to 4–5cm (1½–2in)

● HABITAT
Fairly common on muddy sand and gravelly mud sea beds; lives just offshore

● DISTRIBUTION
Widespread on British coast, but infrequent in south and east

AMERICAN SLIPPER LIMPET *Crepidula fornicata*

The American slipper limpet has a low, slipper-shaped shell. It lives in small chains, with the oldest limpet clamped onto a rock and up to 10 or more living above, on top of one another.

Introduced originally from the United States as fishing bait, this limpet species is now firmly established on all coasts in the southern part of Britain.

● SIZE
Length up to 5cm (2in)

● HABITAT
Usually in groups, in shallow water on rocks and shifting substrata; in estuaries

● DISTRIBUTION
Found on south coast and on southern parts of east and west coasts.

NECKLACE SHELL *Polinices catenus*

The necklace shell is named after the partial rings of eggs that it produces each spring and deposits in sand in shallow water. It has a shiny, almost spherical shell with a low spire.

The necklace shell's outer surface is usually yellowish white with brown marbling.

- **SIZE**
Height up to 3cm (1¼in)

- **HABITAT**
Sandy sea beds

- **DISTRIBUTION**
Widespread and common in southern North Sea, English Channel and western British Isles

BANDED WEDGE SHELL *Donax vittatus*

One of the most common British shells, the fragile banded wedge is roughly triangular in outline and has a serrated inner edge to each shell. The shiny outer surface is yellow and pinkish; the interior may be purple, yellow or orange.

The wedge shell lives buried in sand. It is usually found from the middle of the shore downwards.

- **SIZE**
Length up to 3.8cm (1½in)

- **HABITAT**
Occurs in vast numbers in sandy sea beds close to shore

- **DISTRIBUTION**
Widespread

POD RAZOR SHELL *Ensis siliqua*

The pod razor shell has parallel sides with gaping ends. It is mainly creamy white, finely marked and has a thin outer shell. Its blade-like shape enables live razor shells to burrow quickly in wet sand.

The pod razor shell is commonly found washed up on fine sand with its hinge still intact.

- **SIZE**
Length up to 20cm (8in)

- **HABITAT**
Sandy sea beds from lower shore down to shallow offshore waters

- **DISTRIBUTION**
Widespread

COMMON COCKLE *Cerastoderma edule*

A familiar sight on sandy beaches, the common cockle has a tough, ribbed, almost spherical shell. These shells are sometimes so abundant that they form deep layers on the strand line. Live cockles bury themselves in sand or mud close to the shore.

Each half of the cockle shell has 22–28 radiating ribs.

- **SIZE**
Height up to 5cm (2in)

- **HABITAT**
Sand and silt; most common in estuaries, but also on shores; can tolerate wide range of salinity

- **DISTRIBUTION**
Widespread

COMMON MUSSEL *Mytilus edulis*

Like the common cockle, the common mussel is often collected for food. The dark, deep bluish to purple shell always has a pale yellowish brown mantle edge and a mother-of-pearl interior. Living common mussels are usually fixed to rocks by tough threads.

The common mussel opens only when it is submerged.

- **SIZE**
Length up to 10cm (4in)

- **HABITAT**
Colonies typically found clustered in dense beds on exposed rocks, jetties and outfall pipes

- **DISTRIBUTION**
Widespread

PEPPERY FURROW SHELL *Scrobicularia plana*

Able to tolerate low salinity, the peppery furrow shell is often the only shell that occurs on the upper shores of muddy estuaries. Its valves are thin, quite flat and roughly oval, and are usually white, pale grey or yellow in colour.

The peppery furrow shell provides food for birds and some predatory sea snails.

● SIZE
Length up to 6.5cm (2½in)

● HABITAT
Tolerant of brackish conditions, so able to live in higher reaches of estuaries

● DISTRIBUTION
Widespread

SPOTTED COWRIE *Trivia monacha*

This small, oval shell has a slit-like opening beneath but no spire or point. It is usually pale pink or white and is strongly ridged. The living spotted cowrie's shell is mainly covered by a yellow, orange, red and brown mantle.

Three dark spots on the shell's surface distinguish this species from other cowries.

● SIZE
Length up to 1–2cm (½–¾in)

● HABITAT
Under rocks and seaweed on lower shore and below, feeding on sea squirts

● DISTRIBUTION
Widespread

BLUNT GAPER *Mya truncata*

An oddly shaped shell, the blunt gaper has two shells that appear to have been cut off at one end and never close completely. The blunt gaper is common and long-lived, and buries itself deep in the sand as it matures.

The worn and eroded outer layers of the blunt gaper's shell bear witness to the eroding power of the sand in which it buries itself.

● SIZE
Length up to 7cm (2¾in)

● HABITAT
Lives buried about 20cm (8in) down in sand and mud in shallow water

● DISTRIBUTION
Widespread

GREAT SCALLOP *Pecten maximus*

The reddish brown shell of the great scallop is fan shaped and has a series of radiating folds, each of which is finely ribbed. The lower shell is convex, and the upper one is flat. They are connected by a wing-like hinge.

The living scallop propels itself through the water by clamping its valves together and expelling jets of water.

● SIZE
Length up to 15cm (6in)

● HABITAT
Fairly deep water mainly on fine sand and gravel sea beds, lying in a slight hollow covered with a fine layer of silt

● DISTRIBUTION
Widespread

EUROPEAN OYSTER *Ostrea edulis*

Initially whitish grey, the European oyster darkens into a grey-brown colour and becomes more scaly with age. The shell's exterior is tough and roughly circular, with a flaky surface. The interior has a beautiful mother-of-pearl texture.

The European oyster's ridged shell is often encrusted with tube worms and barnacles.

● SIZE
Length up to 15cm (6in)

● HABITAT
Prefers shallows, but extends to fairly deep water on coarse, muddy sea beds; often covered with fine layer of silt

● DISTRIBUTION
Widespread

Sponges – living sieves

Many of the colourful patches covering rocks and seaweed on the seashore are sponges. They may look inanimate, but sponges are actually colonies of living animals, some of which have surprisingly complex feeding strategies.

The holes in the elephant's ear sponge on the right are the large vents through which water is expelled after the sponge has extracted food particles and oxygen. The beautiful creatures on the left are a colony of hydroids.

Look beneath the tresses of seaweed festooning a rock pool on the shore and you will almost certainly see sponges encrusting the sides of the pool. They 'give' to the touch, like a firm cushion, and are harmless to humans.

Sponges are the most primitive of the world's multi-celled animals, yet they are outstandingly successful, varied and widespread. About 230 species are native to Britain, and most of them live in the sea. The simplest sponges live hanging from crevices or attached to the underside of rocks; the commonest encrust rock surfaces, often in highly coloured patches.

The simplicity of the oganism is illustrated by its structure. The most basic sponge is a collection of flask shapes, each one with an opening at the top called the osculum. The walls have tiny pores through which water is drawn to the central cavity.

SPONGE SUPPORTERS

To survive the buffeting of the waves against the rocks in a shallow sea, sponges have to have some rigid framework to support their cells. Within their tissues, they contain crystalline spicules – tiny pointed spikes – which help protect it. Sometimes the spicules protrude through the surface, giving the sponge a rough texture and making it unpalatable to predators.

Sponges use two principal compounds for their spicules, lime and silica, both of which are easily extracted from sea water. Silica spicules have a thread of protein at their centre, around which the crystal grows; lime (calcite) ones lack such an internal template and are shaped by the way the sponge's cells mould them.

A third sort of skeletal material is also present in some deep-water sponges not found around the British Isles. A tough protein called spongin forms a flexible skeleton which, when cleaned of its living tissues, is sold as a natural sponge for bathing.

Leucosolenia forms many tubular branches, up to 3cm (1¼in) long, with a vent at the end of each branch. It occurs in clumps from the middle shore down to a depth of about 100m (330ft).

Amazingly, when such a sponge is teased apart, its individual building blocks, its cells, re-assemble to form a functional sponge again after a few hours. It seems that each cell can identify its specific location in relation to its neighbours. As they all come together,

cells originally from the outside layer return there while internal cells stick together on the inside.

The internal cells, called collar cells, are the tiny powerhouses of the sponge. Each one has a single thread-like projection, called a flagellum, which beats to create a

◄ The aptly named purse sponge grows to 2cm (¾in) or more and is often found attached to rocks or large brown seaweeds. One of the group with chalky skeletons, its colonies produce larvae each spring and then die.

► In shallow, well-lit water the breadcrumb sponge forms greenish yellow patches over rocks and seaweeds. In deeper water, it is usually orange.

Sponges have little control over where they grow and end up on all sorts of hard surfaces. The size of colonies growing on other animals, such as this scallop, give clues to the host's age.

very weak current of water. The combined effort of all the flagella beating together creates an impressive flow of water through the body. This is the secret of the sponge's success. Together, these microscopic cells can pump water through the body at 10cm/sec (4in per sec), which means that a postage stamp-sized sponge can process a phenomenal 20 litres (4½ gallons) of water every day, from which it takes oxygen and its plankton food.

The coloured sponges are slightly more complex as they have folded walls, creating chambers for more efficient pumping. By beating in the same direction, the whiplike flagella create a strong current to draw more water through the pores and eject it from vents that pepper the surface. The sponge extracts specks of food and absorbs oxygen from the water, and excretes waste products into it, as it flows through.

Reproduction
As they all possess the ability to break up and re-form without a coordinating nervous system, sponges might be expected to reproduce by fragmenting. They do this whenever possible, but

spawning also occurs. Fertilised eggs develop into larvae, which swim in the plankton where they develop into adults – this helps to disperse the species, ensuring sponges are prepared to cope with any long-term changes in their environment.

Predatory sponges
It is remarkable that such a static animal as a sponge can be a menace to shellfish. But one sponge around these shores, the yellow boring sponge, is able to bore into limestone, whether it is in the form of rock or a mollusc's shell. This sponge secretes an acid that loosens small fragments of the rock or shell. These get wafted through the body and lost in the surrounding sea water.

A sponge recently discovered in submerged caves in the Mediterranean Sea has taken this limestone-dissolving

Oscarella is one of the encrusting sponges that spread out over the surface of rocks and seaweeds on the lower shore. The feathery structures are colonies of sea fir, another primitive animal.

process a stage further. It has no internal canals or external vents, but entraps and digests small crustaceans in finger-like projections. It has become an active hunter rather than a passive filter feeder.

Sponges may be the least complex of the multi-celled animals in the sea, yet their simplicity has contributed to their success.

WILDLIFE WATCH

Where can I see sponges?

● Sponges can be found on most rocky shores. Freshwater sponges live in clean rivers and lakes.

● You find sponges well below the high watermark because they soon dry out if exposed to the air.

● Turn over stones and look under ledges in rock pools below the high-tide mark and farther down the shore.

● Look on the surfaces of logs or stones in rivers or lakes for small whitish, brown or green freshwater sponges.

Recognising seaweeds

Whether they form a delicate pinkish fringe in a rock pool or broad green, sometimes brown, bands across the beach, seaweeds of all shapes and sizes are a permanent feature of most shores.

Britain's varied coastline, with its cool waters and a large tidal range, suits many types of seaweed. More than 600 species may be found in the waters of the British Isles.

Seaweeds are large marine algae that are broadly classified into green, brown and red seaweeds. Colour is not always a reliable aid to identification, since some reds have a brownish tint and many browns are olive green.

These relatively simple organisms have fronds of various shapes and many have a robust stem called a 'stipe'. They are not a biologically homogeneous group, however, since the green algae are

plants, but the red and brown algae are not. Most species grow on rocks, stones or other seaweeds, firmly attached by a tough 'holdfast'.

Seaweeds reproduce by means of spores. Having no roots, these algae absorb nutrients directly over their whole surface.

Browns

Seaweeds contain chlorophyll, the green pigment of photosynthesis, which plants use to turn carbon dioxide into sugars and other carbohydrates. In various species of seaweed, however, the green is masked by brown or red pigments, which help these seaweeds to absorb light

and thereby survive in the lower light levels that occur underwater.

Brown seaweeds comprise the largest and most dominant group. They festoon rocky shores and, at the lowest tidemarks and below the level of the tides, form great dense forests several metres tall. They are well adapted to life on the rocky shore. Their fronds are tough and resilient to both battering waves and long periods of exposure to the air when the tide recedes each day. Some have gas-filled bladders that allow the fronds to float and spread out in the water. The various species have adapted to cope with different levels of exposure and

tolerance to drying. As a result, they arrange themselves in distinct zones from the top to the bottom of the shore.

At the top, channelled wrack is able to withstand long periods of exposure to sun, wind and salt. Below that, in order of their decreasing ability to cope with being out of the water, are spiral wrack, knotted wrack, bladder wrack, serrated wrack and thongweed. Around the low watermark, and deeper down in the water, grow the strap-like kelps, which are submerged most of the time.

Greens and reds

Green seaweeds usually grow with fronds that are just one or two cells thick. They are found mostly in pools situated towards the upper part of the shore, often in places where freshwater seeps down from the land and reduces the salinity of the water. The dark green, elegantly branched *Codium* is found in deep pools lower down the shore.

Many red seaweeds occur lower down the shore, and are classic examples of seaweeds that are found in rock pools. For example, neat, forked, slightly iridescent fronds of carragheen (Irish moss) are commonly seen in such pools.

Red seaweeds, such as dulse, also occur in great numbers attached to the stipes of oarweeds, looking rather like ferns on trees in a rainforest.

At low tide, a veritable forest of the kelp oarweed is revealed on the sheltered shores of Scotland's west coast. The broad fronds are supported on long, tough stalks, which can withstand the pounding waves on days when the seas are less tranquil.

DANGER!

Seashores are potentially dangerous places, so always take care. Rocks (and seaweeds) can be slippery underfoot, and trainers, gym shoes or plastic sandals with a good grip are useful. Always check the times of the tides as it is very easy to be cut off, especially where there are cliffs.

EASY GUIDE TO SPOTTING SEAWEEDS

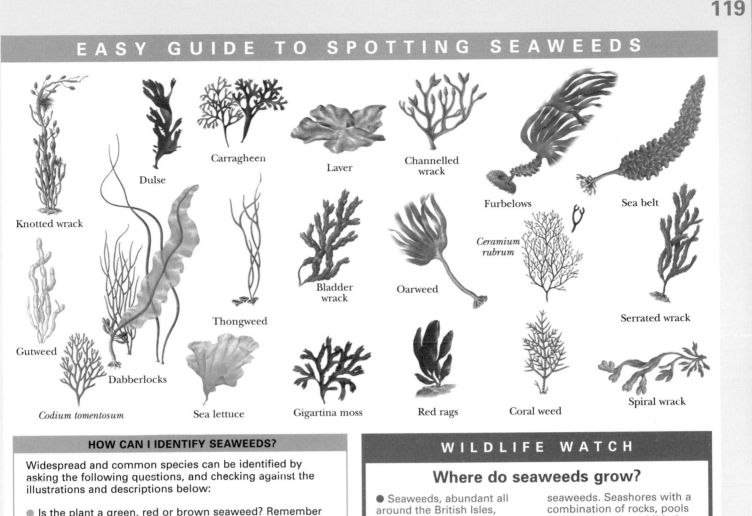

Knotted wrack
Dulse
Carragheen
Laver
Channelled wrack
Furbelows
Sea belt
Gutweed
Ceramium rubrum
Bladder wrack
Oarweed
Serrated wrack
Thongweed
Dabberlocks
Codium tomentosum
Sea lettuce
Gigartina moss
Red rags
Coral weed
Spiral wrack

HOW CAN I IDENTIFY SEAWEEDS?

Widespread and common species can be identified by asking the following questions, and checking against the illustrations and descriptions below:

● Is the plant a green, red or brown seaweed? Remember that reds bleach to brown or green in the sun; and some browns can look greenish.

● Does the frond have a large or unusual holdfast; does it have a stipe (stem)?

● Is the frond broad, narrow, flat, divided or branched?

● Is the frond thick or translucent?

● Does it have any peculiar features such as bladders or warts?

WILDLIFE WATCH

Where do seaweeds grow?

● Seaweeds, abundant all around the British Isles, grow best on the hard rocks of western and northern coasts.

● Look for seaweeds on gently sloping rocky shores, especially where the rocks form natural pools.

● Sheltered shores are often dominated by just a few coarse species, while very exposed shores have few

seaweeds. Seashores with a combination of rocks, pools and sandy areas exhibit the widest range of seaweeds.

● A walk along the strand line after a storm may provide the opportunity to see a variety of seaweeds, washed up by heavy waves. You are likely to find samples of seaweeds that live in deeper water, such as oarweeds and some of the reds.

SEA LETTUCE *Ulva lactuca*

A delicate green seaweed of sheltered shores, the sea lettuce's fronds are reminiscent of sheets of ultra-thin plastic.

When the fronds are not suspended in water, sea lettuce loses its fresh green colour.

● SIZE
Length 10–45cm (4–17¾in)

● KEY FEATURES
Fronds irregular in outline, clear green, thin, wavy, translucent

● HABITAT AND DISTRIBUTION
Common in pools; often grows where freshwater runs on to the shore

● SEASON
Throughout the year; at its best in summer

GUTWEED *Enteromorpha intestinalis*

One of a dozen or so similar species, this green seaweed forms dense floating masses in pools, mainly on the upper shore.

Tufts of gutweed may be found attached to rocks, stones and even limpets.

● SIZE
Length up to 100cm (39¼in)

● KEY FEATURES
Fronds are tubular, pale green, blunt, inflated by bubbles of gas; generally unbranched although several fronds arise from same base

● HABITAT AND DISTRIBUTION
Common in pools high up the shore, especially where nutrient-rich or polluted freshwater runs on to the beach, estuaries and salt marshes

● SEASON
Mainly spring and summer

LAVER OR PURPLE LAVER *Porphyra umbilicalis*

The laver is a red seaweed, displaying a deep rose-pink colour when submerged. The fronds are gelatinous to the touch.

The laver can survive out of the water, but its fronds flatten and blacken when exposed to air.

● SIZE
Length up to 60cm (2ft)

● KEY FEATURES
Fronds irregularly lobed, purplish red but often bleached to greenish brown, membranous and translucent

● HABITAT AND DISTRIBUTION
Widespread on rocks and stones of exposed sandy shores; throughout the shore, often high up

● SEASON
Throughout the year

DABBERLOCKS *Alaria esculenta*

Despite its delicate appearance, this brown seaweed thrives in rocky sites. A distinct midrib distinguishes it from other kelps.

The long, undivided fronds are often split from the edge to the midrib.

● SIZE
Length up to 2m (6½ft)

● KEY FEATURES
Fronds strap-like and delicate borne on a short stalk, which extends as a midrib along the length of the frond; varies in colour from yellowish olive to reddish brown.

● HABITAT AND DISTRIBUTION
Rocks on the lower shore; likes the cool waters of the north

● SEASON
Throughout the year; in south, more noticeable in winter

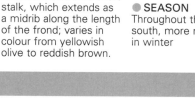

CODIUM *Codium tomentosum*

The tubular fronds of this unusual green seaweed branch in twos and have a spongy, felt-like texture.

The tips of the fronds resemble miniature stag's horns and are surprisingly tough and resilient.

● SIZE
Length up to 30cm (12in)

● KEY FEATURES
Fronds up to 1cm (½in) round, bright green, cylindrical, regularly forked, blunt, with a springy texture

● HABITAT AND DISTRIBUTION
Deep pools on the middle and lower shore, especially on southern coasts

● SEASON
Throughout the year

CARRAGHEEN OR IRISH MOSS *Chondrus crispus*

A bushy red seaweed with tough, flat fronds that divide and form a fan shape, carragheen has a small holdfast and narrow base.

Underwater, the frond tips show a violet iridescence. Carragheen can also appear green in bright light.

● SIZE
Length 8–20cm (3¼–8in)

● KEY FEATURES
Fronds variably stalked, flat, dark or purplish red, regularly forked into fan shape

● HABITAT AND DISTRIBUTION
Common on middle and lower shore and in pools; most abundant in the west

● SEASON
Throughout the year

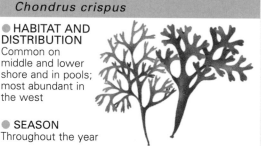

GIGARTINA *Mastocarpus stellatum (Gigartina stellata)*

The fronds of this tufted and much-branched red seaweed are channelled. It often grows in dense stands with carragheen, to which it is similar.

Although a red seaweed, gigartina's colour is altered by prevailing light levels.

● SIZE
Length 7–20cm (2¾–8in)

● KEY FEATURES
Fronds brownish with inrolled margins; dotted with warty reproductive nodules

● HABITAT AND DISTRIBUTION
Common on middle and lower shore and in pools; most abundant in the west

● SEASON
Throughout the year

RED RAGS *Dilsea carnosa*

This distinctive red seaweed has lobe-like gelatinous fronds that are often split towards the tips. Several fronds arise from the same base and short stipe.

At the end of summer, the tips of mature fronds often show hints of yellow or green.

● SIZE
Length 10–30cm (4–12in)

● KEY FEATURES
Fronds reddish brown, often deeply split by wave action

● HABITAT AND DISTRIBUTION
Common in pools and crevices from the middle shore downwards, sometimes in large patches

● SEASON
Throughout the year

DULSE *Rhodomyenia palmata*

Dulse is a branching red seaweed, the fronds of which form an irregular fan. It often grows on the holdfasts of large kelps.

Dulse becomes tougher and thicker with age and size. The frond tips often bear tiny lobes by late summer.

● SIZE
Length 10–30cm (4–12in)

● KEY FEATURES
Fronds with flat, irregular lobes, dark red, thick but somewhat translucent; little or no stipe; the similar *Dilsea carnosa* has thicker, opaque fronds and a short stipe

● HABITAT AND DISTRIBUTION
Common on rocks on the lower shore and on the stems of oarweed

● SEASON
Throughout the year

SEA BELT *Laminaria saccharina*

This large and distinctive brown seaweed has long, belt-like fronds that have a crinkly, crumpled surface. The holdfasts are much-branched.

Sea belt tends to stretch out, flat or half flopped over, whether in or out of the water.

● SIZE
Length 4m (13ft)

● KEY FEATURES
Fronds leaf-like, arising from a short, branched stipe, each flat, yellowish olive, thin and wavy; translucent, with a midrib and side veins

● HABITAT AND DISTRIBUTION
In deep pools or from low-tide level down

● SEASON
Mainly summer

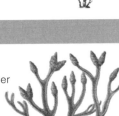

CORAL WEED *Corallina officinalis*

A superficially coral-like red seaweed, the holdfast and lower stipe in particular are calcified and tough.

Coral weed grows in tufts and has a brittle appearance.

● SIZE
Length 3–8cm (1¼–3¼in)

● KEY FEATURES
Fronds fern-like, ranging from yellowish pink and red to purple, but bleaching with age; the regular, slender, bead-like branches stiffen with lime

● HABITAT AND DISTRIBUTION
Common in rock pools, especially low down on the shore

● SEASON
Throughout the year

CHANNELLED WRACK *Pelvetia canaliculata*

Channelled wrack is found high on the shore. Its fronds curl inwards forming a groove along their length in which water is conserved.

The damp channelled side of this brown seaweed's fronds faces the rock; the outer side may look dry and brittle.

● SIZE
Length 8–15cm (3¼–6in)

● KEY FEATURES
Fronds regularly forked, olive-brown (drying blackish), the margins inrolled to form a deep channel; yellow, swollen, gelatinous tips are the reproductive structures

● HABITAT AND DISTRIBUTION
Common on the upper part of the shore at the limit of tides; an unattached form occurs in salt marshes

● SEASON
Throughout the year

BLADDER WRACK *Fucus vesiculosus*

Pockets full of air either side of the distinct midrib lift each frond up towards the light. The fronds are smooth at the edges.

Air-filled bladders and swollen frond tips make this brown seaweed easy to identify.

● SIZE
Length 15–100cm (6–39¼in)

● KEY FEATURES
Fronds branched, flat, olive-brown, with wavy margins and paired bladders; olive-brown, yellowish or orange swollen, gelatinous tips are the reproductive structures

● HABITAT AND DISTRIBUTION
An abundant plant on rocks in the middle part of the shore; an unattached form occurs in salt marshes

● SEASON
Throughout the year

SPIRAL OR FLAT WRACK *Fucus spiralis*

The broad fronds of this common brown seaweed have a midrib and smooth edges. The swollen tips have a rim of flat frond around them.

The clusters of heavy pods at the tip of the fronds are in evidence in late summer.

● SIZE
Length up to 40cm (16in)

● KEY FEATURES
Smaller fronds than bladder wrack and more greenish or yellowish, often slightly twisted and always without bladders; the reproductive tips are yellowish brown

● HABITAT AND DISTRIBUTION
Higher up the shore than bladder wrack, just below the channelled wrack zone

● SEASON
Throughout the year

SERRATED WRACK *Fucus serratus*

Tiny white, spiral shells of spirorbid worms are often seen on the fronds of this distinctive brown seaweed.

At low tide, serrated wrack forms matted masses under which crabs and other marine creatures shelter from exposure to sun and air.

● **SIZE**
Length up to 60cm (2ft)

● **KEY FEATURES**
Fronds similar in outline to other wracks but flat, with saw-toothed margins; reproductive tips are much less swollen. The horned wrack *Fucus ceranoides* has narrower, untoothed flat fronds with pointed tips.

● **HABITAT AND DISTRIBUTION**
An abundant plant on rocks and in pools from the middle shore down to lower shore, forming dense masses. *F. ceranoides* grows in estuaries and land-locked bays

● **SEASON**
Throughout the year

KNOTTED WRACK *Ascophyllum nodosum*

The fronds have no midrib but bear oval bladders. This brown seaweed is often host to *Polysiphonia lanosa*, a red seaweed.

On a rising tide or in a rock pool, knotted wrack floats at the surface, thanks to its built-in buoyancy aids.

● **SIZE**
Length up to 3m (10ft)

● **KEY FEATURES**
Fronds repeatedly branched, flat but thick; dark olive-brown, with tough bladders at intervals; the reproductive structures are stalked, sultana-like and greenish or yellow

● **HABITAT AND DISTRIBUTION**
Abundant on sheltered rocky shores, especially where there is pollution; an unattached form occurs in Scottish sea lochs

● **SEASON**
Throughout the year

THONGWEED *Himanthalia elongata*

The narrow fronds of this brown seaweed are flattened and branching. They grow from the centre of the button-like young plants.

In calm water or in a rock pool, the elongated fronds form tangled mats.

● **SIZE**
Length up to 3m (10ft)

● **KEY FEATURES**
Fronds thong-like, yellowish brown; mature frond grows from the concave centre of young plant; similar bootlace weed *Chorda filum* is longer, darker and lacks mushroom-shaped base

● **HABITAT AND DISTRIBUTION**
Widespread and forming a zone below serrated wrack on exposed shores of southern and western coasts

● **SEASON**
Spring and summer

OARWEED *Laminaria digitata*

It has to be a very low tide to expose oarweed, but whole plants, including the distinctive root-like holdfast, may be washed ashore in rough weather.

The tips of the stalks and the base of the fronds can usually be seen at low tide.

● **SIZE**
Length 1–4m (3ft 3in–13ft)

● **KEY FEATURES**
Stout, flexible, rough stipe; fronds brown or reddish brown, fan shaped, split into strap-like segments; similar cuvie or forest kelp *L. hyperborea* grows lower down, below

low-tide level
● **HABITAT AND DISTRIBUTION**
Common in small groups around and below the low-water mark; best seen at lowest spring tides

● **SEASON**
Spring and summer

CERAMIUM *Ceramium rubrum*

Submerged, this delicate-looking red seaweed resembles a leafless shrub. The branches have light and dark bands, and tiny, pincer-like frond tips.

Ceramium, often found in rock pools at low tide, blends in with other seaweeds.

● **SIZE**
Length 2–30cm (¾in–12in)

● **KEY FEATURES**
Many fine branches, ranging from pure red to dark brownish red; terminal tips of the branches resemble forceps (visible with hand lens).

● **HABITAT AND DISTRIBUTION**
Attached to rocks on the lower and middle shore; mainly in southern Britain

● **SEASON**
Spring and summer

FURBELOWS *Saccorhiza polyschides*

The twisting, wavy margins of the flat stipe, together with the broadly divided fronds, make furbelows easy to identify.

The large, knobbly, hollow holdfast may be home to a number of marine animals, including crabs.

● **SIZE**
Length 1–4m (3ft 3in–13ft); span up to 3–4m (10–13ft)

● **KEY FEATURES**
Frilly fronds growing from a large, flattened, frilly stalk; brown, fan shaped; whole plants washed ashore in rough weather

● **HABITAT AND DISTRIBUTION**
Common but scattered below the low-water mark; mainly on southern and western coasts

● **SEASON**
Spring and summer

Sea-lavender and thrift

Many coastal regions abound with colourful sea-lavender and thrift, native plants that thrive in the salty seaside conditions. Both help to maintain the ecological balance by hindering soil erosion.

Common sea-lavender
Limonium vulgare

Sea-lavenders and thrift belong to the plant family Plumbaginaceae, which is associated with coastal habitats. They are found on sea cliffs, salt marshes and shingle beaches. Thrift also thrives inland on mountains, metal-rich mine spoil, river shingle and lake margins, and sometimes on lowland heaths.

The leaves of these plants are arranged in rosettes around the plant's base, and are usually fleshy and undivided. Numerous small flowers appear in clusters, each flower having five petals. Fused whitish, brownish or lilac sepals, or outer flower parts, support the brightly coloured petals. The fruits are tiny, single-seeded capsules, which are dispersed by the wind.

Sea-lavenders and thrift play an important part in helping to bind and build up the soil in coastal habitats, their lengthy root systems acting as a barrier against the eroding powers of wind and rain.

Thrift is the dominant species of seaside turf, often more or less replacing grasses. In salt marshes, thrift is joined by common and lax-flowered sea-lavender, the three species forming a bright carpet of flowers in summer. In among these species, you may occasionally see some rock sea-lavender, although this is more commonly found in open, sparse plant communities on rocks and shingle beaches.

Diverse thrift

Thrift is one of the more variable species in our native flora; it can be quite small when growing on mountain ledges, while in other surroundings it can grow tall and loose. The leaves vary in hairiness, and the flowers appear in all shades of pink and lilac, as well as plain white. A tall, upright variant with pale pink flowers – subspecies *elongata* – grows on a few inland heaths in Lincolnshire.

From July to late September, drifts of common sea-lavender turn salt marshes in southern and eastern Britain a glorious shade of lilac. The flowers are visited by nectar-feeding insects, such as butterflies, bees, flies and beetles.

Limonium paradoxum

Limonium transwallianum

SEA-LAVENDER FACT FILE

● **Common sea-lavender**
Limonium vulgare
Habitat and distribution
Common in muddy salt marshes, sometimes on rocks, north to the Firths of Forth and Solway; absent from Ireland
Size 20–70cm (8–28in) tall
Key features
Tufted or mat-forming perennial with erect, branched, leafless flowering stems; leaves broadly spear or spoon shaped, in rosettes, long-stalked; flowers bluish lilac, in flat-topped clusters
Flowering time
July–September or later

● **Lax-flowered sea-lavender**
Limonium humile
Habitat and distribution
Widespread in salt marshes and sometimes on muddy sand and shingle north to Galloway and in Ireland
Size 20–70cm (8–28in) tall
Key features
Similar to common sea-lavender, but with flowers in looser clusters, with stem branched more profusely from just below middle
Flowering time
July–September

● **Rock sea-lavender**
Limonium binervosum
Habitat and distribution
Coastal cliffs, rocks and shingle beaches north to Galloway and the Humber
Size 10–30cm (4–12in) tall
Key features
Tufted perennial with slender, erect, branched, leafless flowering stems; short-stalked spear-shaped leaves, 1 to 3-veined, in rosettes; flowers bluish lilac, in erect, spikes, forming flat-topped clusters
Flowering time
July–September

● **Matted sea-lavender**
Limonium bellidifolium
Habitat and distribution
Rare; dry, sandy or shingly salt marshes in north Norfolk and Lincolnshire
Size 10–30cm (4–12in) tall

Key features
Similar to rock sea-lavender, but with many branched, flowerless shoots on lower part of much less erect flowering stems; flowers lilac
Flowering time
July–August

● **Alderney sea-lavender**
Limonium auriculae-ursifolium
Habitat and distribution
Rare; coastal rocks in Jersey and Alderney
Size 10–45cm (4–17¾in) tall
Key features
Similar to rock sea-lavender, but taller, with broader, 3 to 7-veined, spoon-shaped leaves; flowers bluish lilac
Flowering time
June–September

● *Limonium recurvum*
Habitat and distribution
Rare; scattered on coastal cliffs and rocks in Britain and western Ireland
Size 10–30cm (4–12in) tall
Key features
Similar to rock sea-lavender, but flowers more densely arranged and overlapping, spikes spreading or curved outwards
Flowering time
July–September

● *Limonium transwallianum*
Habitat and distribution
Rare; sea cliffs in Pembrokeshire
Size 10–30cm (4–12in) tall
Key features
Similar to *L. recurvum*, but with narrower, spear-shaped, 1-veined leaves and narrow petals that do not overlap
Flowering time
July–September

● *Limonium paradoxum*
Habitat and distribution
Rare; sea cliffs in Pembrokeshire
Size 10–30cm (4–12in) tall
Key features
Similar to *L. recurvum*, but with tiny, 1-veined leaves and short flowering branches, bearing small clusters of 1–3 flower spikes
Flowering time
July–September

As its name suggests, rock sea-lavender prefers cliffs, rocks and shingle banks. Dried, faded sprigs of its flowers are sometimes sold on the street as 'lucky white heather'.

Rock sea-lavender
Limonium binervosum

Lax-flowered sea-lavender
Limonium humile

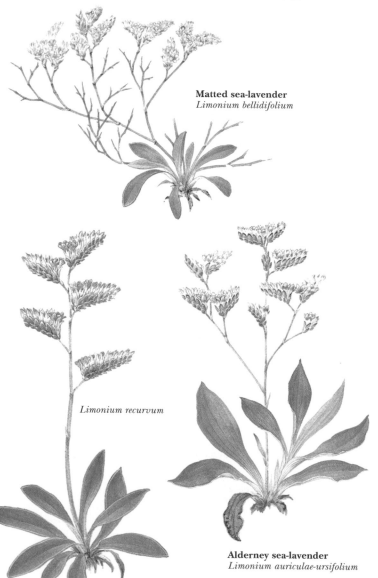

Matted sea-lavender
Limonium bellidifolium

Limonium recurvum

Alderney sea-lavender
Limonium auriculae-ursifolium

THRIFT FACT FILE

● **Thrift or sea pink**
Armeria maritima
Habitat and distribution
Common on cliffs and in salt marshes, on shingle beaches and sand dunes, also mountain grassland, heaths and spoil heaps from mine workings
Size 5–30cm (2–12in) tall
Key features
Mat-forming perennial with erect, leafless flowering stems; leaves narrow, 1-veined, variably hairy, in tufts; flowers purplish pink, in dense, rounded heads, 1.5–2.5cm (⅝–1in) across
Flowering time
April–August, mostly June–July

● **Jersey thrift**
Armeria arenaria
Habitat and distribution
Sand dunes and sandy coastal grasslands around Jersey; does not occur on mainland Britain
Size 20–50cm (8–20in) tall
Key features
Similar to thrift but more robust, with fewer, notably broader and darker green leaves, each with 3–5 veins
Flowering time
May–September

Pink cushions of thrift cover coastal rocks, cliffs and salt marshes all around Britain. Thrift's name may derive from the fact that it thrives, or remains green, all year round.

WILDLIFE WATCH

Where do thrift and sea-lavenders grow?

● Thrift is found along almost all types of coasts. Although it has a long flowering period, its glorious pink blooms are at their best in May.

● Common and lax-flowered sea-lavenders are abundant in salt marshes, particularly in southern and eastern England. Rock sea-lavender is widespread on cliffs, rocks and shingle beaches around Britain.

Jersey thrift
Armeria arenaria

Thrift or sea pink
Armeria maritima

Index

Acknowledgments

Photographs: Front cover Digital Vision, inset Aquila Wildlife Images; Back cover inset Mike Read; 2-3 Woodfall Wild Images; 4 Ardea (J.A. Bailey) (c), FLPA (G. Laci) (b); 5 Mike Read; 6(bl,bc) NP, (br) NP (Paul Sterry); 7 (bl) NP (A.Weston), (bc,br) NP (Paul Sterry); 8 NP (bl,bc) (Paul Sterry), (br) NP; 9 (bl) NP (M.Hammett), (bc,br) NP; 10-11 Biofotos (Heather Angel/Natural Visions); 12(cr) NP (WS Paton), (bl) NP/Paul Sterry, (bc) NP (EC Thompson), (br) Mike Read, 12-13 NP; 13(bc) NP, (br) Natural Visions (Heather Angel); 14(tr) NP (Paul Sterry), (c) NP (Paul Sterry), (b) Mike Read; 15(tl) Mike Read, (tr) NP (Paul Sterry), (bl) Mike Read, (br) NP (Paul Sterry); 16(cl) Mike Read, 16-17 Mike Read; 17(cl) Mike Read, (tr) FLPA, (br) NP (Paul Sterry); 18(tr) FLPA (F de Nooyer), (b) FLPA (E&D Hosking); 19(bl) Premaphotos, (br) FLPA (Tony Wharton); 20(tl) FLPA, (tr) unknown, (b) Premaphotos; 21(t,c,cr,bl) Premaphotos, (bc) FLPA (Julia Swale); 22(tr) Premaphotos, (cl) Woodfall Wild (David Woodfall), (cr) NP (Paul Sterry), (b) NP; 23(tl) NP (EA Janes), (c) Premaphotos; 24,25 Premaphotos, 26 Premaphotos, 26-27(b) NP (TD Bonsall); 27(t) Premaphotos; 28 BC, 28-29(main) FLPA (W. Broadhurst); 29(t) BC; 30-31(t) BC; 31(cl,br) BC; 32(tr) Windrush Photos, (cl,bl) BC, (br) NP; 33(tl inset) BC, (tl) Windrush Photos, (br) BC; 34-35 BC (J Jurka), 35(tl) NPL (A Cooper), (tr) NP (EA Janes), (bl) OSF (R Jackman), (br) BC (A Purcell); 36(tl) Woodfall Wild (Bob Gibbons), (tc) NPL (G de Francisco), (tr,bc) NP (Paul Sterry), 36-37 BC (J Jurka); 37(tr) Woodfall Wild (C.Preston); 38(tl,tr) NP (A Cleave), (cr) OSF (H Reinhard), (b) unknown; 39 Travel Ink (J Swainson); 40-41 BC (Jorg & Petra Wegner); 42(tr) BC (Mark Boulton), (cl) Mike Read; 43(tr) BC (William Paton), (br) BC (Paul van Gaalen); 44(tc) Pat Morris, (c) BC (Gordon Langsbury), 44-45(b) FLPA (W Rohdich); 45(bl) NV (Jason Venus), (c) BC (Paul van Gaalen); 46(tl) NHPA (Laurie Campbell), (cl) NHPA (Hugh Miles), (br) Mike Read; 47(tl) FLPA (W Rohdich), (cl) NV (Jason Venus); 48 OSF (PK Sharpe); 49(tr) OSF (T Shepard), (bc) FLPA (E Hosking), 50(tl) NHPA (S Dalton), (tr) OSF (D Boag); 51(tl) BC (J Burton), (tr) NHPA (S Dalton); 52(tl) OSF (T Shepard), (tr) FLPA (E Hosking), (b) OSF (T Shepard); 53(tl) Ardea (P Morris), (b) OSF (D Boag); 54 FLPA (F Polking); 55(tc) BC (Colin Varnell), (bl) NV (E Lutken & CJ Junge); 57 FLPA (H Clark), 58 FLPA (Silvestris); 59(tl) FLPA (F Polking), (r) FLPA (Silvestris); 60 NP; 61(b) NP; 62(cl,bl) NP (Paul Sterry); 63(tl,cl,bl) NP (Paul Sterry); 64 (tl,cl,bl) NP; 65(tr) NV (Heather Angel), (bl) NP (Paul Sterry); 66(tr) NS (R Revels); 67(tl) FLPA (H Clark); 68(tc) FLPA (A Hamblin), (cr) NHPA (D Heuclin), (bl) NV, (br) FLPA; 69(tl) NPL (MC Wilkes), (tr) BC (Jane Burton), (cr) NS (I West), (bl) FLPA (W Rohdich); 70(tr) FLPA (J van Arkel), (b) NHPA (S Dalton); 71(t) BC (P Kaya), (b) M&C Denis Hout; 72(c) BC (Dr E Pott), (cr) FLPA (J van Arkel); 73 Ardea (JA Bailey); 74(tr) Ardea (J Daniels), (cu) NHPA (M Garwood), (c) Premaphotos, (bc) David Chapman; 75(tc) Premaphotos, (cu) Ardea (J Daniels), (bu,b) Premaphotos; 76(t) W Harris, (cu,b) Premaphotos, (bu) Ardea (JA Bailey); 77(t,cu) Premaphotos, (bu,b) Ardea (JA Bailey); 78(cl) Nick Giles, (b) NP (G du Feu); 79(t) Nick Giles, (cr) NP (N Phelps), (bl) Ardea (P Morris); 80(tr) FLPA (W Wisniewski), (bl) FLPA (J Hutching); 83 BC (Cliff Riedinger); 84 FLPA (G Laci); 85(b) BC (J Burton); 86(tr) OSF (K Wohte), (cr) Sue Scott; 87(tr) BC (T Walmsley), (br) FLPA (R Sears); 88(tr) BC (M Carwardine), (br) Tom Walmsley; 89 BC (J Burton); 90(tr) FLPA (Gerard Laci), (b) FLPA (Pacific Stock); 91(tr) NHPA, (c) NV (Heather Angel), (bc) BC (M Carwardine), 92(tr) NHPA (D Heuclin), (b) BC (J Foote); 93 Aquila (G Smith); 94(br) Aquila (J Need); 95(cl) Aquila (GG & IM Bates), (bl) NV (Heather Angel); 96(cl) NP (M Bolton), (bl) NP (EA Janes); 97(cl) Aquila (M Care), (bl) Aquila (MC Wilkes); 98(tr) Ardea (I Trap-Lind), (b) Mike Read; 99 NHPA (E Soder); 100(tl) Aquila (A Scholver), (tr) Ardea (C Bahr); 101(tl) Mike Read, (tc) Ardea (BL Sage), (tr) FLPA (W Wisniewski), (cl) David Chapman, (c) Ardea (G Knights), (cr) Ardea (H&J Eriksen); 102(tl) NP (A Cleave), (tr) NP (Paul Sterry), (cl) FLPA (G Laci), (bc) Mike Read; 103(t) NHPA (H&V Inge), (b) Mike Read; 104 NV (Heather Angel), 105(t) NV (Heather Angel), (c) FLPA (R Hosking), (b) NV (Heather Angel); 106(t,cu,c,b) NV (Heather Angel), (bu) FLPA (DP Wilson); 107(tr,bl) NV (Heather Angel), (cl,cr,b) NHPA; 108(tc) NV (Heather Angel), (cl,cr,b) NHPA; 109(tr) School of Biological Sciences, (bc,br) FLPA (P Wilson); 110(tr,b) NV (Heather Angel), (c) FLPA (P Wilson); 111(t) NHPA (J Bain), (b) NV (Heather Angel); 112(all) NP (Paul Sterry); 113(t) Marine Wildlife Photo Agency (P Kay), (cu,c,bu) NP (Paul Sterry), (b) BC (Dr E Pott); 114(t,cu,bu,b) NP (Paul Sterry), (c) FLPA (DP Wilson); 115(t,c,bu,b) NP (Paul Sterry), (cu) Sue Scott; 116(t,br) Sue Scott; 117(tl) OSF, (tr) Sue Scott, (cl) NV (Heather Angel), (br) NP (MJ Hammett); 118-119 NV (Heather Angel); 119(cl) NV (Heather Angel), (bl) NP; 120(tlu, tl, c) NV, (cu) Premaphotos, (bu,b) NP; 121(tlu) Premaphotos, (tl,bu,b) NV, (c,cu) NP; 122(tlu,tl) NP, cu,bu) NV, (c,b) Premaphotos; 123 BC (Dr E Pott); 124 Premaphotos; 125 BC (K Taylor).

Illustrations: 19 Ian Garrard (tr); 30 Midsummer Books Ltd; 34 Richard Lewington; 42, 50, 51 John B Ridyard; 54, 55 Midsummer Books Ltd; 56 John B Ridyard; 61, 64, 67 Robert Moreton; 81, 82 Ian Garrard; 85, 86, 87, 88 Sean Milne; 94, 95, 96, 97 Tim Hayward; 100, 101 John B Ridyard; 105(t) Ian Garrard; 109, 112(c) Clive Pritchard; 119(t,br), 120(r), 121(r), 122(r), 123, 125 Ian Garrard.

Key to Photo Library Abbreviations: BC = Bruce Coleman Ltd, FLPA = Frank Lane Photo Agency, NHPA = Natural History Photo Agency, NP = Nature Photographers, NPL = Nature Picture Library, NS = Natural Science Photos, NV = Heather Angel/Natural Visions, OSF = Oxford Scientific Films, PW = Premaphotos Wildlife.

Key to position abbreviations: b = bottom, bl = bottom left, blu = bottom left upper, br = bottom right, bru = bottom right upper, c = centre, cl = centre left, clu = centre left upper, cr = centre right, cru = centre right upper, l = left, r = right, sp = spread, t = top, tl = top left, tlu = top left upper, tr = top right, tru = top right upper.

Wildlife Watch
Waterside & Coast in Summer

Published by the Reader's Digest Association Limited, 2003

The Reader's Digest Association Limited
11 Westferry Circus, Canary Wharf
London E14 4HE
www.readersdigest.co.uk

Reprinted 2004

We are committed to both the quality of our products and the service we provide to our customers, so please feel free to contact us on 08705 113366, or by email at:
cust_service@readersdigest.co.uk

If you have any comments about the content of our books you can contact us at: gbeditorial@readersdigest.co.uk

® Reader's Digest, The Digest and the Pegasus logo are registered trademarks of The Reader's Digest Association, Inc., of Pleasantville, New York, USA

For Reader's Digest:
Series Editor Christine Noble
Project Art Editor Jane McKenna
Editorial Assistant Katharine Swire

Reader's Digest General Books:
Editorial Director Cortina Butler
Art Director Nick Clark

This book was designed, edited and produced by Eaglemoss Publications Ltd, based on material first published as the partwork *Wildlife of Britain*

For Eaglemoss:
Editors Marion Paull, Debbie Robertson
Art Editor Phil Gibbs
Assistant Editor Anne Konopelski
Consultant Jonathan Elphick
Publishing Manager Nina Hathway

Copyright © Eaglemoss Publications Ltd/Midsummer Books Ltd 2003

Printed and bound in Europe by Arvato Iberia

CONCEPT CODE: UK 0133/G/S
BOOK CODE: 630-001-2
ISBN: 0 276 42881 1
ORACLE CODE: 356200001H